Promises to Keep . . .
. . . A Vision for Appalachia

by
Father Ralph W. Beiting

with
Tom Pelletier

Cover Photo by Jeff Rogers

TABLE OF CONTENTS

This book is dedicated to the people all over
America who have sacrificed to generously support
the Christian Appalachian Project and help their
brothers and sisters in Appalachia.

The Christian Appalachian Project
1965-1991

For forty years Reverend Ralph W. Beiting has worked to ease the pain caused by the poverty that afflicts many of the people who live in the Appalachian mountain region. More than twenty-five years ago he founded the Christian Appalachian Project (CAP). CAP is an inter-denominational Christian organization that strives to help people help themselves. CAP provides emergency relief, help with housing, educational programs, business-development programs, and visitation programs for the elderly as well as over sixty other programs and activities designed to bring happiness and peace to those in need.

Through the generous work of thousands of volunteers, hundreds of local workers and a host of loyal donors from all over the country, CAP has become one of the largest relief organizations in America.

PROLOGUE — Friendship

"Ain't you one of them Catholic preachers?"

In the early years of my work in Appalachia, those words were often the prelude to an argument, or at least a confrontation. So when the shopkeeper of a small store where I stopped to buy a soft drink accused me, I immediately bristled.

"Yes I am," I said proudly and firmly.

"Well there's this fellow that comes in here, and he said if I ever did run across one of you fellows to send him down to his house cause he would mightily like to talk to one."

After I got over my surprise, I asked where the man lived and began a journey that taught me a lesson about friendship I have never forgotten.

I wound my way down route 421 across a creek to where the hill called simply "Big Hill" began to stretch out. There, in a tiny, run-down cabin I met a man named Jesse and his wife Maggie.

Almost immediately, as if he were confessing, Jesse told me he had recently been in prison for moonshining.

He explained that some years back, the small shack next to his cabin had become a moonshine marketplace. At first Jesse ignored it, but every night there was noise and commotion "til the wee hours," so eventually he called the police.

The police came and broke up the moonshining operation. The moonshiners got off easy and a few days later they returned to Jesse's house. They knocked on the door and said they wanted to make up with him and be friends. They plunked down a jug of moonshine whiskey as a peace offering and then left a few minutes later. Not more than two or three minutes had passed when the state police showed up and arrested Jesse for possession of unlicensed liquor—a federal offense.

That, at least, was Jesse's story. In any event Jesse found himself at the federal prison at Ashland, Kentucky. There he was befriended by a young priest who visited the inmates regularly. In his frequent talks with this priest, Jesse took the first steps on a long walk toward God.

When he got out of prison Jesse lost touch with the priest, but he hadn't forgotten what he had learned and experienced about God. That was why he told the storekeeper to keep a lookout for another one of those "Catholic preachers."

Over the next three months I visited with Jesse and Maggie every Monday night to talk about God and the Bible.

Maggie was shy at first. On my first visit she went into the bedroom and closed the door. The second time she did the same, except that she left the door open. The third week she said she had to do the dishes so she stayed with us in the kitchen. The fourth time she was firmly settled in the chair next to the potbellied stove. After that we were great friends, and she often had a meal waiting for me when I got there. I sat at their rickety table and noticed they had put large cans under the table legs so they wouldn't go through the rotten floor boards.

Finally, after several months of visits, Jesse surprised me. "I want to be baptized," he said. "I'm nearly 75 years old, and I've never been baptized before, but I'm ready now."

A week later, I baptized both Jesse and Maggie in the small hall I was using as a church. When the simple but powerful ceremony was over, Jesse went outside and presented me with a beautiful, hand-carved cane.

It must have taken him months to whittle the intricate designs that covered it.

"Father, this is for you," he announced.

I looked at him and thought of his poverty and the amount of work that went into creating the cane and answered, "I can't take that, Jesse. You could sell that for a great deal of money."

A pained look came over his face and I could see that I'd greatly insulted him.

"If I can't give you something in return for all you've given me, then how can we be friends? If I can't thank you, then how can we really care for each other?"

Standing there with Jesse I learned that helping people can never be a one-way street. I learned that friendship which doesn't return friendship doesn't really exist.

I have never forgotten what Jesse taught me. That's why I hope that, by writing this book, I can return something to all the people who've helped me in my work and help the people of Appalachia return something to the generous people all over the country who've helped them.

Promises to Keep

The woods are lovely, dark, and deep,
But I have promises to keep,
And miles to go before I sleep,
And miles to go before I sleep.

Robert Frost, from *Stopping by Woods on a Snowy Evening*

This past year I almost gave up and ended my ministry and my part in the Christian Appalachian Project.

Those of you who know me or who read my book, *Appalachia . . . a Special Place . . . a Bridge of Hope,* know that last January I was nearly killed when I fell asleep at the wheel of a van I was driving and plowed into the rear of a fully loaded coal truck.

I was pinned in the truck with a broken leg, broken arm, broken nose and several other injuries. Worst of all, the van caught on fire and was in danger of exploding with a full tank of gasoline.

Luckily, and by the grace of God, I was saved by a fire truck that happened to pass by at that moment. The fire fighters stopped and put out the fire and I was painfully extracted from the van after more than two hours of effort.

I spent the next six weeks in and out of hospitals and convalescent homes recovering from my injuries. My recovery did not go smoothly.

The doctors originally thought I had a simple crack in my left wrist. Ten days and a great deal of pain later, they discovered that my wrist was not actually broken. A small bone that was out of place was causing the excruciating pain.

A few weeks later I needed an operation to repair my crushed nose. It had been set after the accident but my interior nasal passages were still constricted and I had a hard time breathing and speaking.

I was supposed to be in the hospital overnight for this "routine" surgery. At 6:00 o'clock the morning after the surgery, however, I began to hemorrhage, and they had to operate again. I lost eight pints of blood, and doctors told me that I was actually lucky to be alive; I had come very close to bleeding to death.

Finally, after six months, I felt as if I were healthy enough to get back to work on the many projects I had going. One of those was to build a chapel for a small community along the Tug Fork River that separates Kentucky and West Virginia.

The Catholic community in that area had once had a church dedicated back in 1925. In 1978 the church had to be destroyed. Over the years dirt and mud slides on the opposite side of the creek that ran adjacent to the church had slowly but surely brought the water closer to the church. Finally winter rains and snows caused a large slide that forced the waters of the creek over its bank, and it raced through the church.

The damage was too much to repair, so the parishioners reluctantly gave up on their beloved church. They acquired a double-width mobile home and converted it to hold services.

I promised I would help them build a new, more suitable place of worship. After we hired a bulldozer and had a foundation poured, I needed to inspect the work and bring some building materials to the site. Since the accident, I usually had friends drive me where I needed to go since I didn't feel up to driving myself, but this day I couldn't find anyone so I decided to drive myself.

In retrospect this was not a good idea. A few days earlier I had experienced pains in my left side. My doctor had told me they were caused by a serious hernia. He was able to temporarily stop the pain, but he suggested I see a surgeon the very next day. I had several commitments for the next day, and the day after that, and the day after that . . . so I put it off and made an appointment for a couple of weeks down the line.

As I was driving to the church site the pain returned and got worse with every mile. I thought about pulling over and getting help, but I figured if

I could just make it to the church, I could rest and I'd be all right.

After what seemed like an eternity, I pulled the van up to the little mobile-home church and got out. I made it as far as the makeshift altar before I collapsed from the pain. Hard as I tried I could not get back up. I prayed that someone would come by the church and rescue me.

Fortunately, some women of the church found me a short-time later. They called a local doctor (a phone had been installed just two days earlier). He determined that I needed to be operated on that afternoon and I was driven to the hospital near Paintsville where I live. The operation took place that afternoon.

It was my sixth operation in a year. Thanks be to God it went well, but I was wearing down, physically, emotionally and spiritually.

I have been near death three times this year. Even after all the surgery and all the medical attention, I have one hand that is only about 50 percent functional. I have bad vision in one eye, continuing problems with my back and painful arthritis. In addition to my physical suffering, I was mourning the loss of a brother who passed away just a month before the accident.

That's when I almost quit.

I started to ask myself—and God—why I should go on. I was 67 years old and past the age at which Catholic priests normally retire. I had worked hard all my life and accomplished many things. I was tired and sick.

"God," I said, "why are you making this so hard on me all of a sudden? Haven't I done enough already? Do I have to go on and on forever?"

I thought about just exploring and enjoying the mountains I love so much, without responsibilities, without pressures. I thought about traveling to the many other lovely parts of the country that I've seen over the years. I thought of having more time to study the Word of God and to read other good books.

It all seemed so lovely and peaceful and quiet — so tempting.

While in the midst of this mood, I scanned my bookshelf and my eyes fell on a collection of poems by Robert Frost. Robert Frost has always been one of my favorite poets, but I was very busy. To this day I don't know why I stopped to read that book. As I read, I came to the poem called, "Stopping by Woods on a Snowy Evening" — one of my all-time favorites. I read the poem eagerly, still not quite knowing why, until I came to the final verse:

> *The woods are lovely, dark, and deep,*
> *But I have promises to keep,*
> *And miles to go before I sleep,*
> *And miles to go before I sleep.*

Suddenly it all became clear to me. The woods are certainly "lovely, dark, and deep." It would be lovely to retire and take life easy. But I have "promises to keep" before my life ends. And "miles to go" before I'm ready to quit.

As I thought about this I felt God reaching me with a message. I had a strong feeling that He was saying to me, "If you really want to help people, and if you really want things to go more easily, why don't you stop fighting me and let me lead you?

"All these years you've been telling me what you're going to do and how you're going to do it. Why don't you be quiet and listen for a while? Why don't you pay attention? Why don't you let me show you the best way to do things?"

I thought about the gospels. I thought about Jesus, the man who had preached as no one had ever preached before, a communicator with no equal in the history of the world, a man who had the power to work miracles and even bring the dead back to life. He was a man who inspired loyalty as no else ever had or ever will. He had extraordinary personal power.

Yet, as the end approached, He said to His disciples, "Only when I am lifted up on the cross, only then can I draw all people to myself."

I think He meant that in order to succeed, He had to give more than His energies, His talents, and His power. He had to give Himself. That was the highest expression of love and the most powerful act possible.

I think that's what God was saying to me. He was asking me if I were ready to endure and suffer and walk with Him the "miles to go before I sleep." He was telling me that the way to help save His children here in Appalachia was to give up my own ambitions—my plans; give up "my" projects and truly start listening more to what He wants done. Only when I can do that will I be able to keep the promises I made 40 years ago to the people of Appalachia.

I hope in my vocation I have not been primarily advancing my own desire for fame and recognition. I have throughout my life tried to do what I thought God wanted. But I'm human. I'd be a liar if I denied that I enjoy personal success and recognition. I think God was asking me to try harder than ever to lose myself in His will.

A couple of weeks ago, we had a reunion of the teachers who had taught at the school we started in Paintsville, Kentucky more than 45 years ago. One of the teachers brought a picture of me when I was just 22 years old. At first, seeing this picture reminded me of my troubles with age. In the picture I had black hair; I was much thinner; I was big and strong and confident. I could swing a hammer all day and carry children on my shoulders and leap small buildings with a single bound. I was Superman.

I was also a young man with a dream to change Appalachia.

Now I'm 67 and hurting. My hair is white; I've gained too much weight. I can still swing a hammer but not for long, and if I tried to put a child on my shoulders I'd probably throw my back out.

I still have the dream, but I'm not Superman anymore.

Maybe that's good. Back then I didn't rely on God's help enough. I prayed for His guidance certainly, but I felt, in the optimism and power of youth, that I could do it all.

Over the years, I've accomplished some of what I dreamed but not nearly enough. Now it's time to let God take over. If I let Him use my talents and my remaining strengths He can accomplish more in a few years than I have accomplished in forty.

So I will keep going. There is much left to do. I hear God saying to me, "The foxes have dens and the birds have nests, but the Son of Man doesn't always have a home and my children don't always have a place to rest their heads."

I am still tempted by the vision of an easy retirement. I can't deny it. But the truth is that I'm glad I can't quit. I don't want to watch from the sidelines as God renews the people of Appalachia. In my heart, I know He is going to do it with or without me. I want to be involved. I want to pray, and work, and walk the extra mile.

In this realization I feel both peace and urgency—peace that I may, for the first time in my life, be truly giving myself up to God for the people of Appalachia and urgency because I know the end of my voyage is nearing. The light at the end of the tunnel grows brighter with each year that passes.

I have a lot of promises to keep. As St. Paul said so beautifully, "Charity, the love of Christ, urges me on like a spur in the side."

I hope you'll join me as I walk the miles to go. There are few satisfactions greater than to keep a difficult promise. There is no denying that the promises we have to keep are difficult. There are still people in Appalachia who sleep in shacks. There are still far too many adults who can't read or write. There are still children who go to bed hungry and cold. There is still too much loneliness and pain and sickness.

This past year I nearly gave up. But I will never quit until all the people of Appalachia have hope in the future. I have "promises to keep."

A Promise to Volunteers

Two roads diverged in a wood, and I—
I took the one less traveled by,
And that has made all the difference.

Robert Frost, from *The Road Not Taken*

I don't think any writer has ever captured as
well as Robert Frost did in this poem, the critical
choice facing all human beings in their lifetimes—
to do the easy thing . . . or do the right thing.

Robert Frost wasn't writing about volunteering
specifically, but his words apply perfectly. To give
freely, without hope of reward or recompense, is
what volunteering means. It isn't easy. It's far
easier to follow the other road and ignore the
needs of humanity. But the greater joys of life lie
down that road less traveled.

When a person volunteers to help the people of
Appalachia by coming here to live and work with
us, or just as importantly, by generously support-
ing our work, I make them a promise.

What do I promise volunteers here in Appalachia? Certainly not money. Not fame. Not ease
or even popularity. My promise to volunteers is

that they will find peace—the peace of Christ.

Last summer I worked alongside a young woman from Minnesota. Sue had volunteered to help us for a few weeks. I realized that she was a wonderful worker, full of the love of Christ. I'm sure that at the time she figured she was fulfilling her duty as a volunteer and that she could then go back and continue her career as an accountant. Sue had taken a few steps down the hard road, and now she was going back to the well-traveled road to easy, sure success.

But I couldn't let her off that easy. I pointed out the other road. "You ought to quit that job and come down here to live," I said. "You could do something special here in Appalachia." I suggested she talk with Mike Sanders, one of our directors.

Sue wouldn't commit herself and sort of brushed me off. In her mind she was already on that other, easy road. But the "less traveled road" kept beckoning. A few weeks ago I received this letter from her:

Dear Father Beiting,

I started a letter to you just a few weeks after I had returned from Paintsville, but I got side-tracked and never completed it. I trust you have recovered from your hernia surgery. I pray that God keeps your health so you may continue doing His work for the people of Appalachia.

Shortly after I got home I read your two books, *Appalachia . . . A Special Place* and *God Can Move Mountains,* and was deeply moved. I could imagine you telling those stories. It was like hearing you talk again when I was reading.

I want to thank you for putting me in touch with Mike Sanders before I had to return to Minnesota. I was surprised to hear myself tell him that I would think of volunteering next summer. I was surprised because I hadn't yet consciously decided to respond to what I felt I was being called to do. I still consciously consider myself exploring the possibilities. Even now that I have decided to respond to the call for volunteers, I wonder if I'm responding to my will rather than God's. I guess I should trust Him to take care of it either way.

Anyway, good luck and God Bless you in the next few months' efforts in Appalachia. I pray that your organization's call for volunteers will be heard in the hearts of many so that the wonderful work being done in God's name can continue strongly.

God Bless,
Sue

Now Sue has stepped off the well-traveled road onto the one less traveled. I know she'll never regret her choice. And I know Appalachia will be a better place because of her choice.

When I was a young priest, sent to Appalachia

to serve the few Catholics that lived there, I also saw two roads in front of me. One was the calm, quiet, well-traveled road of parish priest. I could look forward to a life of ministering to my small flock, saying Mass seven or eight times a week, and retiring at age 65. My biggest concern would have been how to manage the parish budget.

That was the road I initially planned to follow. But when I came to Appalachia and saw the poverty and suffering all around me, I saw the other road.

The other road was not well-traveled. In 1950 there were very few people concerned about the needs of Appalachia's downtrodden. If I were to follow the road of caring and working for the poor, I would face hardship and indifference. I would face long, long days of hard work followed by sleepless nights. I would face the widespread animosity toward Catholics and especially priests. I would face the hardest suffering and despair.

I don't think I saw all those things down that road, at first, but knew I was looking at a much more difficult journey than that of a normal parish priest.

I took the second road and have never looked back.

At first I didn't think of myself as a volunteer — just a man with a dream to do as much as possible for the poor.

When my neighbors came to my door asking for

food or clothing or other help, I did whatever I could. I drove back home to where my family and friends lived in Northern Kentucky, collected donations, then drove back to Appalachia and distributed them. I thought I could solve everyone's problems this way.

One night I was driving back home to our church in Berea. As I reached a place called Bobtown, about five minutes from home, I suddenly got a sick feeling. I realized that I wasn't a hero, accomplishing great things. I was a truck driver. The food I had collected would be gone in a few days; the clothing would wear out in a couple of months. None of it would make any difference to the people who received it or to the communities where they lived.

I don't know if I have ever felt so futile as I did that night.

Nevertheless, out of that despair came an idea that created the Christian Appalachian Project. It wasn't until my ego was crushed that I suddenly realized I wasn't the only person who could help the people of Appalachia.

It finally dawned on me that there must be hundreds, thousands, maybe millions of Americans who would volunteer to help their brothers and sisters in Appalachia if they only knew of their plight.

From that point on my dream ceased to be wishful thinking and became a possibility.

I thought, "What if I talk to people and write to people and ask them to volunteer?"

All kinds of possibilities would open up. Some could volunteer their lives. They could come and live here in Appalachia and dedicate themselves to serving the people every day as I had. Others could volunteer their hard-earned and much-needed resources. They could send money, or clothes, or books. Others could come and visit for a while and help build a church or a home or befriend a poor family to help them build a new life of hope.

Everyone could play a part—some big, some small. God has given us each a special talent, needed here in Appalachia. I was confident that the beauty and generosity of America would win out.

That's the moment when the Christian Appalachian Project was born. In the years since that day, my vision has been vindicated a thousand-fold. More than 40,000 people have volunteered their time here. Many more have sent money—some a few dollars, some thousands.

All of them have found that the more they gave, the more they received. Once you begin to give, the desire to give grows and grows until the giving begins to hurt, and that's when it means the most. In the Bible, Jesus tells us that the woman who came to the temple and gave her last few pennies did a far greater act than the rich man who gave thousands.

Years ago, I said something to a group of volunteers that has become sort of a capsule philosophy of volunteering with CAP. At the end of a very long day some volunteers told me they were exhausted. I said to them, "Well, tired volunteers are happy volunteers."

Nowadays, whenever a group of volunteers are especially tired at the end of a day, they will look at each other and say, "We certainly are happy today, aren't we?"

I firmly believe in that philosophy. We have had volunteers who simply wanted to talk about good works. They would debate for hours about the needs of Appalachia and the correct social and theological policy for curing the ills of the poor. One day I had heard as much as I could stand.

"Let's stop talking," I said. "Let's get out and get busy. Let's visit some people. Let's build some houses. Let's walk the valleys and meet the poor. Let's wear out the soles of our shoes. Then we'll accomplish something.

"No one ever met the needs of these people with talk. If we don't join our hands to our voices we are just wasting time."

I don't think the young people I was admonishing appreciated what I said right then, but sometimes it's necessary to prod even the most dedicated volunteers lest they lose sight of their own goals. A while ago, I received a letter from a young woman who once resented me for this very much:

Dear Father Beiting:

This letter is long due you. Perhaps you don't remember me. I was only one of the long line of volunteers through the years, but I need to ask your forgiveness.

In 1980 I was a volunteer at Mt. Vernon, living at the Quarry Street House. I was immature in my relationships and I did a lot of arguing. You pulled me aside and told me that I had to change my focus, and that I should move to the volunteer program in Lancaster.

I didn't want to leave the Quarry Street House where I was comfortable and had friends. I resented your decision, and when I left CAP six months later I was very bitter.

Once out of the situation I was able to straighten up my life and get my priorities right.

Now eight or nine years later the Lord has brought this all back to my attention. I cannot be pure and holy as He is holy with this sin in my life. And so I ask your forgiveness for holding bitterness against you, and for causing disunity among volunteers. For this I am truly sorry, Father Beiting.

About ten months after I left CAP, I married a man who had been a missionary in England for four years. We have three children, Joshua, six, Rachel, four, and Abigail is two.

We have heard the call of God in our lives. In June of next year we hope to be ready to leave for

Lynndale, Texas where we will spend six months in an intense course on missionary training along with lessons in Spanish. After that, we are off to Venezuela.

Again, please forgive me and I pray for you and CAP and that God will continue to bless it and you.

In His love,
Michelle

This letter brought tears to my eyes because I know I am hard on volunteers sometimes; not because I want to be hard, but because I know that people need leadership and that our work is so urgent here. But I'm human. Often I wonder if I'm being too hard, or that I will make them resent and dislike me. Most of all I worry I will turn them off to volunteer work or, even worse, to God's call in their lives.

To hear this young woman tell me after all these years that she is still following God's call to mission work and that she no longer resents my direction made me feel that it is all worth it.

Choosing "the road less traveled" is not easy. Our Lord Jesus gave us the greatest example of that in the garden of Gethsemane. He was innocent of any crime or sin. He could have walked away from His mission with a clean conscience, but He chose to die for us all. His was the greatest act of volunteerism ever committed.

Luckily, that kind of sacrifice is not required of us to help the people of Appalachia. That was a road that only Jesus could walk. But there are many other roads we all can walk — quiet, country roads in Appalachia that lead to families in great need, lonely elderly people, and hungry children. Those are the roads "less traveled" that you and I can walk.

I have one more letter to share. It is from a woman who has been a tireless volunteer with CAP for many, many years. She no longer volunteers because she has been promoted in her work and cannot leave her new responsibilities. She still manages to convince others to come and volunteer, though. Each year she sends a van full of eager young people. Each year I send them back to her exhausted . . . and happy.

She writes:

Dear Father Beiting,

I dreamed of you this week and took that as a sign to write you. In my dream there were two scenes. In one you were being compassionate to a little girl and helping her and her family. In the second you and I were standing at the end of a paved road that went nowhere. We gazed out over a large valley of healthy green trees with a blue sky above.

In my dream I felt excited to be on an unfinished road with you looking out into a vast area of possibility and growth. It reminded me of all the summers I worked with you and of all the good we did together.

Good Luck in one more new beginning. With Fond memories,

Sister Sue

The hardest part about being a volunteer is that sometimes you don't see the fruits of your labor immediately. You could really use that money you just donated, or you feel the fatigue from working all day to repair the house of a poverty-stricken family, or you are depressed by the loneliness and decrepitude of an elderly woman's life. Without seeing the effects of your sacrifice, it becomes hard to keep putting one foot after another on that "road less traveled."

The rewards are there even if you can't see them. The donation does matter; the friendship does matter . . . the love does matter.

A while ago I visited Emmaus House in Berea. This had once been a motel, before I purchased it and turned it into a home for the elderly. Here those who can no longer live at home can have dignity and companionship.

I was asked to come and share a meal with the residents. When dinner was finished, I got up to say a few words, and after a couple of minutes I couldn't think of anything else to say. This is a rare occurrence for me, to say the least. I was

flustered for just a second or so, and then I had
the inspiration to ask the elderly residents if they
had anything to say.

For what seemed like an eternity, there was
silence. I was beginning to think I had blundered
and embarrassed both myself and these wonderful
folks. Then a woman timidly raised her hand.

"I'm 90 years old," she said. "I lived in Mount
Vernon. I remember when you first came and I remember the people you brought with you. I have
no children of my own, but all the people who
visited me over the years and sat at my kitchen
table have been my family more than I ever could
have dreamed. They warmed my home; they gave
me a purpose for living, and they gave me joy."

She went on to describe special times she had
spent with CAP volunteers, how much she looked
forward to hearing the knock on the door when
they would visit and how much they helped her.

When she had finished, my eyes were misting almost as much as hers.

Then another woman got up. She said, "You
know, I lived all by myself out in the hills, and I
have no relatives or family in the whole state. And
I got right scared at night—I never opened my
door. One night some boys came onto my front
porch. They pounded on my door and one of
them said to open up because he was my cousin. I
knew I had no cousins so I wouldn't open the
door, but I was mightily scared. I sat there all night

wishing I had someone, family or friend, with me who could protect me and help me. The next morning I saw a car drive up, and it had that CAP symbol on the side—that rainbow with the cross. I knew it was volunteers from CAP. I knew that someone special had come. I opened my door and said, 'Come friends. Come.' It felt so beautiful to be able to say that."

When she was done speaking there were hands up all over the room. One man told how volunteers had helped him learn to read and that he found such joy in it now. Another told how volunteers had comforted him when he was sick and thought he was going to die. Others told how volunteers had driven them to doctor appointments, or played cards on the kitchen table, or brought seeds to help grow a garden.

This went on for nearly an hour and when it was over and the room was silent there wasn't a dry eye in it.

This kind of love is the result of taking "the road less traveled" . . . it makes all the difference.

The Promise of America

Something we were withholding made us weak
Until we found out that it was ourselves
We were withholding from our land of living,
And forthwith found our salvation in surrender.

Robert Frost, from *The Gift Outright*

The people who settled this country were brave fools. They left the safety of their mother countries in Europe, set out on dangerous sea voyages, and tried to build homes in a new land where nothing was guaranteed and death lurked around every corner.

It was a foolish idea, but they were driven by something undefinable: the need to be free and to profit from their own drive and determination. They came to America because America was the land of hope and opportunity. America was the land of promise.

I've always thought that the greatness of America's accomplishments stems from the fact that only the bravest, most self-confident people had the courage to settle this distant and dangerous land. They left us a legacy of courage.

When things became too comfortable in the colonies, another group of men once more hit the road, pushing the search for opportunity even further. They came to the seemingly impenetrable Appalachian mountains and settled in the valleys and hills. These are the ancestors of the Appalachian people.

A few years ago I wrote a book about these bravest of the brave; men like Daniel Boone, George Rogers Clark and Isaac Shelby. There wasn't anything these people couldn't do. They built their own houses, made their own clothes, made gunpowder and bullets, nails and plows.

When Americans desired even more freedom and made the decision to cut the ties to the British crown, the people of Appalachia were on the front lines. I honestly doubt that America would have won the War for Independence if it hadn't been for the heroic leadership of Daniel Boone, if it hadn't been for George Rogers Clark leading his brave men across the endless miles to capture key British forts at Vincennes and Detroit, and if it hadn't been for all the other valiant efforts of the Appalachian people.

Did ever a land begin with such courage and determination—and hope—as did Appalachia?

Today that hope is largely gone.

The other day I was at one of our offices when a woman came in to plead for a loan to pay her electric bill before the electric company shut off her power. I wandered away to give the woman privacy as she explained her plight to our outreach worker. When I looked out the window, I recognized a pickup truck that had been there several times recently. A man of about thirty-five or so sat glumly in the driver's seat, staring at his shoes.

I suspected it was the woman's husband so I went out to chat with him.

"It's a lot warmer inside," I said, motioning to the door. He pulled his collar up over his neck, forced a smile and shook his head, "I'm all right, thanks."

I stayed there for a minute, wondering why I hadn't had the sense to put my jacket on before venturing outside. I watched my breath float away in white puffs.

"Well, if you won't come in, how about if I come in there with you?" I asked with a shiver.

This time his smile was a little broader and he leaned over and opened the door.

"My name's Father Beiting," I said as I shook his hand.

"Ron," he replied with the forced smile again.

"Good to meet you, Ron," I said again through chattering teeth. It wasn't much warmer in the truck than outside.

"What's your last name?"

Ron stared at the windshield for a long time. Finally he told me.

He turned away from me and pretended to be

interested in the snow that had begun to fall. I
watched a red bloom of frustration and shame
spread from the back of his neck, through his
cheeks and finally surface in the corner of his eye.
He buried his face in his hands. They were big and
rough.

"Have you been out of work long?" I asked.

"Four months," he said when he could speak.
"Ever since the factory closed. Worked there
eleven years—don't know nuthin' else. No one
else will hire me."

He gripped the steering wheel tight and leaned
back in his seat. "I don't remember being so
ashamed in all my life," he sighed. "I chop wood,
run errands, haul trash, mow yards and I still can't
pay the bills."

We talked for several minutes more. I asked him
if he would come back when he could. I told him
I'd like to help him find work.

He never did come back, and his family moved
away. I hope and pray they are all right.

To people like Ron, the promise and hope of
America is a story of a foreign land in a fairy tale.
They wonder why they are left out. They begin to
say, "What's wrong with me?"

We've come a long way from the land of hope.

In some ways, I feel America is holding back her
promise of hope from Appalachia. And in the poem
"The Gift Outright," Robert Frost says, "Something we are withholding is making us weak."

America needs Appalachia, we can't be whole . . . we can't be what we've been called to be without it.

The people of Appalachia are cut off from the promise. Today I see so many young people in the mountains who have no hope for the future. They don't see any value in even trying. "What difference does it make?" they ask me.

For a long time, Appalachia relied on the coal industry for its economic strength. Today, the coal industry is declining. But other areas of America have had their primary industries decline and found new sources of growth. The Northeast, for example, was once heavily dependent on mill work. Today the mills are almost entirely gone, but the region is still integrated into America's economic mainstream. Somehow America built a new economy and a new promise there. Why hasn't that happened in Appalachia?

I think America owes Appalachia another chance. I don't believe she owes Appalachia a handout—I fight the idea of dependence with every bone in my body. But America needs to look to the mountains and see a great untapped resource here that can make us all stronger.

That's why I constantly write to our supporters and to people in positions of power telling them about the forgotten people of Appalachia. Some people resent this. They ask me why I'm always pointing out the negative aspects of Appalachia.

They have a point and it's very true that there are pockets of hope in Appalachia. Those pockets of hope are exactly why I am so driven. I want to see all of Appalachia share in the opportunity that defines America.

The pioneer spirit that found its greatest expression here in these mountains isn't dead. The American dream isn't dead. It just hasn't been tried in the last hundred years.

Today, the challenge is not to conquer an untamed land but to conquer poverty and illiteracy. Today the danger comes not from Indians or wild animals but from the greatest tract of uncharted despair in America.

I believe that America is the greatest nation on earth, because we rise to challenges. In fact, we seek them out just as our ancestors did when they left the safety of their homelands.

The greatest challenge America faces today is poverty, and where better to tackle it head on than in Appalachia?

Some time ago a man named Abraham Lincoln grew up here in Kentucky. He went on to serve his country and his homeland by declaring that America was one people, not half with and half without. We need new Lincolns today—people who will reunite Appalachia to America and bring the promise home again.

God's Promise to Humanity

I turned to speak to God
About the world's despair;
But to make bad matters worse
I found God wasn't there.

God turned to speak to me
(Don't anybody laugh);
God found I wasn't there—
At least not over half.

Robert Frost, *Not All There*

"I think you are missing the purpose of your life," my good friend Lou said to me a few days ago. We were sitting in a darkened room, lit by a single candle flickering on the table. Lou and I had been discussing my work and the work of CAP and this very book. His statement shook me.

"What do you mean by that?" I asked him.

"Well, I don't mean to say that you haven't done a great deal. You've built churches and homes for the elderly and schools and camps for the children. You've created jobs for the poor and disabled. You bring food to people at Christmas and all that.

"Yet I look at you and wonder if you aren't wasting your time.

"God gave you talents and God gave you life, and God spared your life on numerous occasions this past year. What are you going to do about it? You write books that are interesting and full of little stories and challenging ideas, but what you do best is talk about God. Why don't you write more about God? You have promises to keep in Appalachia. What about your promises to God?"

It took me several hours to fall asleep that night as I thought about what Lou had said. I think he was right. I'm going to try to take his advice and I want to dedicate this chapter to him.

God IS the key to all that we do. I often preach that to the people who volunteer for CAP. But as much as I say it, I think I still sometimes forget it myself. As Robert Frost says in the poem that begins this chapter, sometimes God is speaking to me and I'm just not there.

A month or so ago I received a call from a man who manages a social service agency charged with caring for the poor in Martin County. He wouldn't tell me why he wanted to see me but it sounded important, so I agreed to visit.

We sat in his office and when I asked him why he wanted to see me, at first he tried to change the subject. Finally it all came spilling out. He told me that ten years ago he lost God. He saw the way the world was going, the poverty and injustice and violence, and he couldn't understand how a just God could allow the world to be like this. He said, "I guess I'm an atheist now."

I said nothing, waiting to see what he wanted from me.

"In the last few years I've begun to feel that maybe I was wrong—that maybe I've made a terrible mistake. Every day I meet with poor people. They come here with nothing, no education, no job prospects, no security for the future. They have little food or clothes and no money. When I try to find solutions to their problems we often meet a dead end. There seems to be no hope, no end to the misery. I get depressed . . . but strangely enough, they often don't.

"They tell me, 'Don't worry, at least I still have God. Everything will work out in the end. God won't forget me.'

"At first I used to laugh at them. It seemed like such a foolish idea. What had God ever done for them? But as the months go by, I find that even with all the good things in my life, I can't find real joy or contentment. I'm beginning to wonder if I'm not the one who is poor and they aren't the ones who are rich.

"I have money, and security; they have God.

"I saw your name in the paper and I asked around and people said you were a man who cared. I'm hoping you'll care about me. I want to believe again. Will you help me find God again?"

Somewhere in the middle of this speech the man had begun to cry and now he sat there, broken . . . tears streaming down his face.

I told him I thought that of all the virtues, honesty is the one that God loves most. He was being honest in saying that he thought God had forgotten, had walked away and left the world in the hands of villains. He was being honest in saying that he thought he had made a mistake.

I reminded him of things that were deep in his own heart. I reminded him of God's goodness— that God is not a God of hate or war or injustice. In fact, He sent His only Son to end those things.

In a small way, I think I helped him open his heart back up to God.

We talked for 45 minutes or so and promised that we'd talk again. Since then I've sent him books that I've found helpful in my own walk with God. I hope he will find God again soon and will hear God call to him, "Come home My son."

I received a phone call one evening last week. A muffled voice requested, "Father Beiting." I asked how I could help.

The man on the phone told me he had been looking for a job for weeks without success. He was 400 miles from home and he was down to his last few dollars. He was so depressed he couldn't sleep. In desperation he had looked in the phone book for a minister and found my name. I could tell by his voice that he was stretched to the emotional breaking point.

"What can I do to help you?" I asked him.

I expected him to tell me he needed a place to sleep, or food, or gasoline for his car. His request surprised me. "Would you pray for me?" he said softly. "I think I need God more than anything else. I'm so lonely."

We talked for 15 minutes or so. I assured him of God's love for him. I told him God was eager to be a part of his life and that God would never leave him orphaned.

When we had talked for a while he said, "Could you pray for me now?"

I don't know when I've ever put more heart into a prayer than I did at that moment. When the "Amen" came the man was in tears.

"Thank you, thank you, thank you," he said. "I feel that God is with me now. I think I can try and go on again."

I have not heard from the man since but I was struck by his simple faith. The prayers we said meant more to him than food, money or shelter. I can picture him as one of those in the Bible who wanted nothing more than to touch Jesus' robes. All he wanted was to be close to God.

God is faithful to His children, but we need to be ever ready to serve as His messenger. I am honored that I was chosen that night to bring God's love to a man who desperately needed it.

Several days later I received another call. The phone rang at 11:30 at night and I jumped out of bed to answer it. Once again, it was a young man. He told me he was at the Carl Perkins Rehabilitation Center five miles out of town.

The young man said he was from Harlan County. He had serious back problems from an injury he suffered while in the military. He was at the Rehabilitation Center learning new job skills so he could find a decent job.

"Is there anything you need," I asked him.

"Oh, I don't need any physical help," he said. "I am well cared for here. What I want to know is, can you help me find God?

"I am 21 years old and something is missing. I don't know what it is, but I had a dream the other night and in my dream an angel tried to talk to me. I woke up before he could speak, but I think it was a sign that God is trying to enter my life.

"When I asked around at the Center, people said I should talk to you. I was afraid to call at first because I'm not a Catholic and I thought you might not want to talk to me. I've been struggling with this for days now, but a few minutes ago I decided I would call you and take a chance. Am I calling too late?"

I assured him that a call like his could never come too late. I told him that because of his courage God was now closer to both of us.

I have begun visiting the young man frequently

and we are exploring his faith and the Good News of Jesus. I look forward to my visits with him, and I am struck once again that with all the problems this young man faces in trying to build a new life with his disability, he would call me and ask, "Can you help me find God?"

He reminded me that all our struggles, all our searches, must begin with the struggle and the search for God's purpose in our lives.

In my own heart I know I am not always as open to God as I could be. I pray that as the years go by and I get closer and closer to the day when I will meet God face to face, I can be more open to Him.

I think back to my friend Lou's remarks about my work, and I know that it is important that we make God a part of our everyday lives and our work. Too many people want to hold God captive in church. They are perfectly happy to let God lead the way during church services. But when it comes to the marketplace, or the highways and by-ways, to our daily relationships with the people around us, God just seems to get in the way.

If you look at the life of Jesus, you'll see that his work was not exclusively religious. Many of the miracles he performed affected everyday concerns. He fed the hungry, he cured disease, he restored children to their parents. In His first miracle at Cana He simply changed water into wine.

Our God, when He came to earth, was busy

with the living of people's lives.

That tells me our God wants very much to be a part of this world. He wants very much to live with us every day. He has promised us that if we turn to Him, He will answer. Jesus said, "Ask and you shall receive."

That's a pretty strong promise.

But God will enter our lives only when we ask Him. One of the greatest gifts God gave us is the freedom to choose to follow Him. With His great power He could make us all slaves instantly. None could defy Him.

Instead, He waits patiently for us to ask Him into our lives. There is war and suffering and injustice . . . not because of God, but in spite of God, because we haven't asked Him to join us. We're the ones who have defiled this paradise.

This morning I was struck by an example of how this affects Appalachia. I read in the paper that the governor of Kentucky announced the expansion of a large manufacturing plant in Kentucky. The expansion will create 1,500 new jobs. I'm glad of this new economic development for the state, but I'm distressed that it will be built in an area of the state that is already booming with prosperity.

Here in Eastern Kentucky and throughout Appalachia we have empty factories. Within a few miles of here there is a factory that once made excellent tents. Another empty factory once made shoes, still another turned out fine clothing. To-day, they no longer welcome the workers who once found a livelihood here.

I wish a few of the wheeler-dealers in Washington and in our state capital of Frankfort would put their minds to bringing industry to the mountains where it is really needed.

I don't begrudge the rest of Kentucky its success. I'm a Kentucky boy through and through, and I'm proud of the state as a whole. But I know there are wealthy people, in Kentucky and around the nation, who would invest here in Appalachia if they opened their hearts to God's calling.

God has promised His people in Appalachia that He wouldn't abandon them. I know He has put out His calls to those with business and financial resources. So far, there haven't been many answers. That's why Appalachia still suffers with crushing poverty.

The truth is that if someone told me to invest a million dollars for the greatest return, I wouldn't invest it in Appalachia either. As much as I love Appalachia and her people, I know far too many other places where a greater return could be made on an investment. But there is more to life than profit, and how can we begin if no one is willing to take a risk and accept the fact that a reward may not come tomorrow?

That's why I made a personal commitment in 1991 to reach out to business people in Kentucky and around the U.S. I'm working to amplify God's call a bit so that maybe they'll hear it.

I've formed an interdenominational group of religious people to approach business and financial leaders with concrete proposals to create new businesses and employment in Appalachia. We're not going to lie and tell people they will get rich. We're going to present it as a far greater challenge.

We're asking people to search their hearts and listen to God and discover if, perhaps, He wants them to invest in Appalachia, not for profit necessarily, but for love.

This may seem like a pretty foolish idea in our secular, mercenary society. But sometimes foolish ideas are the best. And God's foolish ideas are a million times more wise than the wisest ideas of humanity.

Remember in the Bible when the prophet called forth one of the Jewish judges to lead an army to cast off the yoke of Israel's oppressors? The judge raised an army of tens of thousands. The prophet looked at him and told him to send the army home. He said God would win this battle with only 300 soldiers. Talk about a foolish idea. Then the battle began and the enemies of Israel, numbering in the tens of thousands, were crushed.

Was there ever a boy more foolish than David? King Saul was being handily defeated by the Philistines. They sent their giant, Goliath, out to meet the Israelites. He cursed them and dared them to send a warrior to fight with him to the death. Not one of Israel's bravest soldiers could summon the courage to face him.

Finally God moved a young boy, a teenager, to volunteer to fight Goliath. David couldn't even wear armor because no suit was small enough for him. He went forth with a few stones and a slingshot. Was there ever an idea more foolish?

We all know what happened.

I would love to see people with business and financial acumen move here to Appalachia and set down roots here. It's a wonderful, beautiful land. I challenge anyone to find an area of the United States more blessed with natural wonders.

Come here to join us. Bring your families. Together we can create a new future. Imagine the satisfaction you'll gain. I'm not talking about the satisfaction of designing a new product or a new market. I'm talking about building a new future for a lost segment of American society.

I wish all those who can't come would help in other ways. Even those who are bedridden, or dying of cancer, or suffering in other ways, can offer their prayers and suffering for Appalachia.

As sure as the sun will rise tomorrow, God will hear those prayers. Ours is not a God of pain and suffering. He is a God of love. He alone can turn pain and suffering into love.

I can already hear the business people and the bureaucrats saying that bringing business to Appa-

lachia won't work. They'll say it's crazy. Just like
sending a boy out with a slingshot to fight a giant
is crazy. They'll see.

God has never broken a single promise He's
ever made. None of us can make that claim.

He promised us He will be our God if we'll be
His people. He said, "I will bind your wounds; I
will feed you when you are hungry; I will give you
drink when you are thirsty; I will be there when
you need me; I will never forget you."

Jesus asked His disciples, "Which one of you
when your son asked for a fish would give him a
snake? How much more shall your Father who is
in heaven give what is good to those who ask
Him!"

If we will only surrender to God's will and ask
His help in our lives, there is nothing we cannot accomplish.

A few years ago I came across a story called
"Footprints." No one seems to know who wrote it
or even where it originated, but I dearly love it.

FOOTPRINTS

There was a man who died, and he reviewed
the footprints he had taken in his life.
He looked down and noticed that all over
the mountains and difficult places that he had
traveled there was one set of footprints;
but over the plains and down the hills,

there were two sets of footprints,
as if someone had walked by his side.

He turned to Christ and said,

"There is something I don't understand.
Why is it that down the hills and over the smooth
and easy places You have walked by my side;
but here, over the tough and difficult places, I
have walked alone, for I see in those places
there is just one set of footprints."

Christ turned to the man and said,

"It is that while your life was easy
I walked along your side;
but here, where the walking was hard
and the paths were difficult,
was the time you needed Me most,
and that is why I carried you."

God will carry us if we let Him. Like the man
who told me he had lost His God, we must all
work to find Him. If we do, there is nothing that
will stand in our way. God has promised. He will
not abandon His people in Appalachia. I know in
my heart that's a promise He will keep.

Promise to the Peacemakers

Before I built a wall I'd ask to know
What I was walling in or walling out.

Robert Frost, *from Mending Wall*

One day two thousand years ago, Jesus sat down overlooking the Sea of Galilee and gave the greatest sermon ever. Today we call it the "Sermon on the Mount." In that sermon He said, "Blessed are the peacemakers for they shall be called sons and daughters of God."

That's quite a promise. It's also quite a challenge. I suspect that human nature has more natural aggression and violent tendencies than it does peacemaking tendencies. I think the history of civilization—including the war in the Persian Gulf—bears this out.

I think we can overcome this nature and be peacemakers if we only stop to think of the idea that Robert Frost expresses in his poem, *Mending Wall*. If we stop to think before we construct the many walls we put up in our own lives, between friends, between husbands and wives, between the rich and the poor, between black and white, be-

tween the old and the young, I think we'll find it a
lot easier to be the peacemakers Jesus calls us to
be.

I know I have a great deal of trouble with being
a peacemaker. I'm the kind of person who tends
more toward confrontation when something or
someone stands in the way of a goal I want to
reach. Whenever I find myself slipping toward
those tactics—which only build walls between
us—I remember Jesus' quiet promise, "Blessed
are the peacemakers for they shall be called sons
and daughters of God."

For forty years I have tried to instill this idea in
the Christian Appalachian Project. In my last
book I talked about building bridges between
God's people. That is essentially a mission of
peace.

Today there is a great deal of room for peacemakers to operate, both here in Appalachia and in
the rest of the country as well. Our divorce rate is
astronomical. Spouse abuse and child abuse are
far too common. Strain between races and socio-
economic groups threatens to erase the gains of the
civil rights movement.

Yes, there is a great opportunity for a few good
peacemakers.

This is especially true in Appalachia where families have so many strikes against them and must
contend with poverty on top of all the normal
stresses of life.

One day years ago I visited a young man who was in prison. His father remembered me and remembered CAP from the time we helped him repair the roof of his barn after a tornado. He called and asked me to go talk to Eli.

Eli sat there in his jail cell and stared at the wall when I introduced myself. I remember that I was weary and hungry when I went to see him. I didn't really want to be there, but I had promised Eli's father I'd see him.

I told Eli that I cared about him, and he told me to get lost. I told him Jesus loved him — he told me to get lost. I told him I would pray for him. I told him he wasn't alone and that Jesus could help him if he asked Him to. Again and again Eli told me to get lost.

I finally gave up and went home discouraged and exhausted. So much for peacemaking.

I didn't recognize him at my front door nine years later. He stood there with a bag of groceries and asked, "You remember me, preacher?

"I was in prison and you visited me."

I couldn't place his face but his words echoing the Bible raced through my memory down to my soul: "I was in prison and you visited me."

As I struggled to remember who he was, he told me that he didn't have time to talk, as he was on his way to see his parole officer.

"Maybe these will help somebody else," he said as he pressed the groceries to my chest.

By the time I realized who he was, his car was out of sight and all that remained was a bag of groceries and the distant roar of a bad muffler.

I guess sometimes the peacemaking we do isn't obvious at first. When I met Eli, my concern seemed to bounce right off the anger, hate and scorn with which he walled out the world. But somehow, with God's help, peacemaking words managed to find the cracks in Eli's mortar. After nine years he still remembered that solitary visit. The peace of Christ found its way to his heart and grew until Eli could no longer contain it. It now flowed out of him to reach into the lives of others.

The peace Jesus promised us works like that.

An elderly man named Tom thought he was beyond Christ's peace. I stood beside him one day staring at the smoldering remains of the old shack that had been his home.

Burnouts are such a common catastrophe among the poor of Appalachia. Ramshackle houses and old mobile homes with poor wiring, heated by coal or wood, are just fires waiting to happen.

"Maybe you should just go and help somebody else," he told me. "I'm too old and tired. I just don't have it in me to rebuild."

It was a while before I could talk. What could I say to an old man as he stood before the ashes of his life? Everything he owned had been in that little house.

Finally, I put my hand on his shoulder and said, "Why don't we just pray for now? We'll deal with the rest later."

We stood there amid the ashes and prayed. We asked for courage. We asked for strength. We asked for comfort and support.

When we were finished Tom's eyes smiled at me from behind a flood of tears, "I guess I ain't really lost everything, have I?" he cried.

We began from that prayer—and together, one plank, one nail and one day at a time we built a new house and put his life back together.

We were able to help Tom build a new life on the ashes of his old life. I wish it always worked out that way, but the truth is that just as often our efforts to bring peace are more like Eli's story than Tom's. Even so, every person who is a part of CAP—each supporter, each volunteer, each dedicated employee—is a peacemaker. They all deserve to be called sons and daughters of God.

Another of CAP's programs is our Family Life Center which serves families in distress, of which there are far too many in these lovely hills.

There can never be a good excuse for beating a spouse or a child, but I know from day-to-day experience that the pressures of poverty and despair, and the destruction of self-esteem that follows them like the plague, push many otherwise good men and women over the edge.

Family Life Services helps pick up the pieces of

these very unpeaceful families. We give women a safe home while they try to find help to save their marriages. We can't instantly heal the wounds, and we can't instantly put a marriage back together, but we can help spread a little of the peace of Christ to a battered woman or child.

Last fall the small community of McKee, Kentucky was in desperate need of peace.

Panic surged through the town as news spread that a young man had pulled a gun at school and was holding thirteen children hostage. People who knew the young man said he was extremely troubled by his parents' divorce.

The poor boy was acting out his rage at his very unpeaceful world. I don't know why he thought that killing someone would make his life better or less painful, but we human beings do very strange things when Christ's peace is missing from our lives.

Throughout the town, parents clung to each other for comfort, wondering whether they'd see their children alive at the end of the day. Finally, as night fell, the boy gave up his gun and his captives.

The crisis was over, but the boy had transferred his hurt to other children. His pain remained like a silent ghost, haunting the school corridors, the buses and the homes of the children.

I think this tendency of pain to spread from one person to others is one of the greatest causes of evil in our world. That's why we try so hard to bring peace and stop the hurt before it spreads.

CAP's Family Life Office counselors worked long hours over the next few weeks to try and bring Christ's peace to the children and their families. For more than a month, we worked with each child stricken with fear or anger. We met with families and talked with groups of students. We couldn't erase the memory of that terrifying day, but we were able to heal many emotional wounds and drive out fears.

I was extremely proud of the work our counselors did—they were true peacemakers and children of God.

Sometimes spreading the peace of Christ is as simple as giving someone a hug, or a kind word, or reading a book to an elderly person.

I remember a couple who used to come to our church. This couple should not have had peace in their lives. They were dirt poor. They lived in a converted tool shed behind a friend's house. Carl's mother was ill and needed constant care. His wife Sheila was dying of Hodgkin's disease. It had left her blind and unsteady.

But their simple faith and the friendship of a Christian community brought them a rare and treasured peace. Since Carl was illiterate and Sheila could no longer see, they would ask for volunteers to read the long letters they often received from their daughter in Ohio. Carl and Sheila would hold hands as they listened to news of their daughter's life. Then they'd dictate a letter back, always asking at the end, "Did you put down that we love her?"

CAP sold them a used car so they could make it to doctor's appointments for both Sheila and Carl's mother. They diligently paid us back; five dollars here, three dollars there.

Within a few years, Carl lost his mother, his wife Sheila and even his daughter, and yet Christ's peace continued to comfort him. He told me, "I can always feel the hand of God on me. I felt it when we lost Mom and all the while Sheila was sick, and when she lost her leg and when she died. I felt it again when I buried my daughter beside them.

"I ain't alone," he swore, "I ain't alone."

I think that's the key to Christ's peace. When we stop building walls around ourselves and around others; when we let Christ into our lives through the people we reach out to, that's when true peace comes to us and never leaves.

It's not easy. Strange as it seems, it's easier to build those walls than to tear them down. It takes a lot to say, "I need help" or "I'm sorry" and even more to say, "I forgive you."

But there is a great reward for this struggle. It's no small thing to be counted as a son or daughter of God.

Over the years I've had the humbling privilege

of seeing a great deal of generosity flow from donors and volunteers to the people we serve. If I had to choose from all the wonderful gifts we have been able to extend to the people of the mountains—houses for the homeless, food for the hungry, work for the unemployed, and so many others—if from all these fine programs I had to choose the one gift that holds the greatest hope for Appalachia it would be the peace of Christ.

I thank everyone who has helped bring that peace. You are truly sons and daughters of God. And when I die and they bury me here in these mountains I love, I hope that I will be remembered with the simple phrase: "He spent his life in the mountains, and he made peace."

If my life can rate that simple statement, Jesus has promised that I will be called a son of God. There can be no greater ambition.

A Promise to the Children

How Love burns through the Putting in the Seed
On through the watching for that early birth
When, just as the soil tarnishes with weed,
The sturdy seedling with arched body comes
Shouldering its way and shedding the earth
  crumbs.

Robert Frost, from *Putting In The Seed*

Whenever I read this poem of Robert Frost I think of the children of Appalachia. I imagine them, the seeds of our future, rising up with straight backs and strong values through the weeds of generations of neglect, shouldering aside the poverty and despair of their parents and grandparents, building a new Appalachia of hope.

A few weeks ago I was saying Mass at our little church in Paintsville. Like most Catholic services ours was quiet and reverent, except that there was a little boy, about three years old, who kept escaping from his mother and running around the church. He was having a great time, squealing every time his mother caught him. Finally, at the quietest point in the service, when everyone was silently meditating, he escaped again and came directly up to the altar.

It was the time after Communion when we all sit down and silently talk to God. The little boy walked right up to me, so I put an arm around him and pulled him onto my lap. He came without hesitation and immediately quieted down. We sat peacefully for several minutes. The congregation was spellbound. They knew this was not the usual course of the service and many people feel the noise and commotion children make during Mass is a hindrance to quiet worship.

On this day, however, I think we all felt that in that little boy we had God in our midst.

The little boy sat there, enjoying the attention, but not realizing that he was affecting us all so. I could sense that he felt safe, bathing in the special kind of love emanating from the room full of adults surrounding him.

He stayed beside me the rest of the service and after it was over he and I walked hand-in-hand down the main aisle to the back of the church.

His mother came up to me and apologized profusely, but I said to her, "Please, please don't apologize. This was the nicest thing that has happened to me during Mass in a long time."

It made me think of when Jesus was surrounded by children and the apostles tried to shoo them away. "Let the children alone," He said to them, "and do not hinder them from coming to Me; for the kingdom of heaven belongs to such as these."

Another time Jesus said, "Unless you become like children, you shall not enter the kingdom of heaven. Whoever then humbles himself as this child, he is the greatest in the kingdom of heaven. And whoever receives one such child in My name receives Me."

Those words of our Lord remind me that of all the promises we make to the people of Appalachia, the most important are those we make to children.

These promises are not different from the promises humanity makes to every child on earth—that you will be loved, you will have a chance to develop your full potential, you will have the opportunity to succeed.

Unfortunately, in Appalachia these promises are harder to keep than anywhere else in America.

That's why CAP's programs for children are the most important of all. In our child development centers, summer camps, Bible camps, teen centers and school programs, we try to instill three things in children—self-confidence, a love of learning, and most importantly, a love of God.

Last summer I visited one of our Bible camps. The children were learning about Jesus and how He was crucified. A boy of about seven stood up and proclaimed, "You mean those ornery buggers put Him to death when He was so good. I'd sure like to meet one of those guys, I'd give him a good one!''

Now, of course, we don't teach or condone violence, and we weren't really trying to get him angry at the men who put Jesus to death. Someday, when he's older, he'll learn that we all share responsibility for that atrocity. But it was delightful to see this child's naive and valiant love of Christ. Maybe if we all loved God as decisively and completely, we could collectively give evil ''a good one!''

Sometimes we wish children would grow up and be more like adults. I wish we adults could be more like children—trusting, full of faith and optimism for the future.

The truth is that the future for most of Appalachia's children is pretty bleak. Too many of them will learn despair and the futility of struggle at their parents' knees. They'll give up trying before they are out of their teens. They'll accept that life means getting by, collecting a welfare check, or living off someone else. They will never try their wings.

That's not what we promised them.

There is a young Appalachian woman named Francie whom I have known since she was three years old. Her mother had six children, by several different fathers. The fathers of her half-siblings were no great shakes, but Francie's father was the worst. Rather than support her as a father should, he abandoned the family. The only time Francie saw him was when he'd stop her on the street to ask her for money.

Her mother has her own problems. In fact, she is presently in jail for public intoxication. Hers has been a life of wantonness, drunkenness and child neglect.

We first met Francie when she came to one of our child development centers more than 17 years ago. She was a bright and capable kid.

She had, by the age of three, spent so much time baby-sitting her younger siblings that she was adept at changing diapers and cooking macaroni.

She knew all her colors. The sheriff's car was brown, the state trooper's car was gray, and the social worker's car was blue.

She could count. "One bill don't mean nuthin," she'd say. "Two bills mean you gotta find the money somewhere. Three bills mean they cut the lights off."

This child was three years old — a three-year-old adult! Is this what we promised our children?

We did all we could to give Francie a real education and at the same time let her be a child while she was with us. When she was in fifth grade her mother took off to Columbus, Ohio, with her latest boyfriend and left Francie and her five brothers and sisters with Francie's grandmother.

There Francie's education continued. She learned how to buy a month's worth of groceries, with $27 worth of food stamps, and how to spend the stamps quickly before her uncles took it from her to trade for beer.

She learned to sleep under her bed because she had more room than if she slept on top with her brothers and sisters. She learned to forge her grandmother's signature when teachers sent notes home saying she'd fallen asleep in class.

Francie somehow survived this "education."

When she was fourteen she received the "Outstanding Achievement" award at our summer camp. I can still remember her smile that evening. Every day her grandmother told her she was lazy, stupid, a liar and a thief. But that night we all told her that she was decent, honest, bright as a whip, and full of potential.

I had hoped that the encouragement we gave Francie would stay with her, but it seemed we couldn't compete with the daily realities of her life and her family. In her senior year of high school, Francie began to believe her grandmother. Her grades dropped. She started lying and staying out late. Counselors at the CAP teen center talked with her for endless hours without success.

When graduation came around that spring, Francie had failed and she decided she would quit school. No matter how much we talked to her she said her decision was final. We all began praying for Francie, praying that she would reverse her decision. Still she told our counselors that she was done with school. We continued to pray.

When fall rolled around and school started, Francie was there. I believe that Jesus answered our prayers and led her back.

This coming spring Francie will graduate, at the age of 20. Now she has applied to the University of Kentucky. When she talks about college she has that same smile she had when she received the "Outstanding Achievement" award at our summer camp.

So maybe we have kept at least some of our promises to Francie. She now believes in herself, and she has the beginnings of an education. The rest is up to her, but I know that any child who could do what Francie did at age three has unlimited potential. I keep her in my prayers.

Keeping these promises we've made to our children isn't easy. I often wonder where we'll find the food to feed them at our child development centers. I wonder where we'll find good teachers, where we'll get enough desks and books and supplies.

But a promise made to a child should never be broken. So we keep going, sometimes in the dark, to make sure we do everything we can. I think children are worth going into the dark for.

I often tell that to girls who come to our Family Life Services shelters because they are unwed and pregnant. I try to counter all the advice that says, "terminate your pregnancy, it's the simplest way out." That is never the right solution. It breaks our promises before the child ever sees the light of day.

It robs the unborn child of the chance to know the unsurpassed joy of a hug from a loving parent, to see a sunset, ride a bike, to make a mark on the world. Many women who come to us are indeed unable to care for a child. They are too young themselves, or lack the financial stability to care for a baby. But there are hundreds of thousands of families across the country who can't have children, who pray daily for a chance to love a baby and to keep the promises.

Parents are the key to our promises to children. We try to fill in the gaps, and we do everything we can to support parents, but we can never make up for them. I am very optimistic for Francie, but it makes me terribly sad to imagine what kind of a young woman she might have been if her parents had the ability to love her. She would be a super-star today.

That's why CAP works so hard with parents. We visit struggling families to help them find ways to work out their problems. We hold weekly meetings where parents can talk to each other and grow and learn from each other.

Most of all, children need and want love from their parents. In America today we give our children far too much of everything but love. We give them money and fancy clothes and Nintendo games . . . but when it comes to love, the checking account seems to be empty.

In Appalachia, our parents are often unable to love their children because of drug or alcohol abuse, or because they must work three jobs to make ends meet. In our child development centers we try to provide some of the love children miss at home. We also expect that parents work at least two days a month at their child's center so they can learn more about parenting and contribute to the education of their own child.

Usually the parent who shows up is the child's mother, but I'm happy to see that in one of our centers a couple of fathers have volunteered to help out. Most of all, Appalachian children need good male role models. Too many fathers are gone from the home, or are alcoholics or abusive.

Larry is a truck driver. He lost his job a while back and hasn't been able to find another. His wife is going to school trying to build a career, so he comes to work at the child development center. He says he's happy to call himself "Mr. Mom" as he takes care of his own children and the children at the school.

All the children love him and look up to him as a surrogate father.

Another man, Glenn, was disabled in an accident a few years ago. He took up the traditional—and traditionally female—Appalachian craft of quilt making. He comes to our child development center twice a month and teaches the kids to sew and do other crafts. He helps the kids shed old ideas about male occupations and about disabled people.

These two men are helping keep the promise to the young children of Appalachia.

When I was a young priest I took a great delight in children. I loved to carry them around, sometimes four or five at once. I have been proud to see many of those children grow into responsible, loving adults with children of their own. I have seen too many others, to whom the promises weren't kept, go down different, darker paths. I mourn for them every day of my life.

Today, these legs are no longer able to keep up with young children, but I love them no less. I am even more committed to keeping the promises we've made to them. I will not rest until every child in Appalachia has a chance to grow healthy and strong in mind, body, and soul.

I may not live to see the children I meet today grow up and have children of their own. But I know if we keep our promises to them—if we love them above all else—they will grow up to be like the seedlings in Robert Frost's poem. They will stretch above the weeds of poverty and shed the crumbs of despair. They will build a new Appalachia, a better America . . . a new promise.

The Promise of a Friend

When a friend calls me from the road
And slows his horse to a meaning walk,
I don't stand still and look around
On all the hills I haven't hoed,
And shout from where I am, "What is it?"
No, not as there is a time to talk.
I thrust my hoe in the mellow ground,
Blade-end up and five feet tall,
And plod; I go up to the stone wall
For a friendly visit.

Robert Frost, from *A Time to Talk*

Just before Thanksgiving last year I received a call from Judy, a CAP worker. She took me to visit an elderly woman named Emily.

We got off the state road and wound around large mud puddles as we crept down a narrow dirt road. There at the end of the road, under a tree by a creek, stood Emily's trailer. It was 8 feet by 30 feet and it looked simply awful. All the windows had long ago been broken out and replaced with plywood and I could see holes in the aluminum skin that covered the sides.

Just before we went inside Judy warned me to watch out for holes in the floor. If I could have seen inside the trailer, I would have taken her advice but it was so dark I could have missed the Grand Canyon. Luckily, I didn't put my foot through a hole—and I got to meet Emily.

While we introduced ourselves I looked around in the dim light. The boards on the windows kept out some of the wind I guess. But since the boards shut out the sunlight and Emily had no electric lights, it also made the place seem like a cave. If it weren't for small beams of light sneaking through the holes in the siding and the walls, it would have been completely black.

A sheet of plastic was taped and nailed up to the ceiling in an attempt to keep the roof from leaking. It wasn't even marginally successful. Leaking water had rotted the floor.

Because the trailer was too decrepit to pass electrical codes, Emily had no electricity, which meant no lights, no refrigerator and no water pump. She had a tiny kerosene heater that did its best to keep off the late fall chill, but it didn't burn well and gave off terrible fumes.

"It burns my eyes sometimes," Emily told me, "but I hates to be cold."

Emily told me she hauled her own water up the hill from her nearest neighbors. It was hard work for an old woman and water was precious to her— she used it very sparingly. Consequently, her home

Except in cases of emergency, CAP tries to avoid handouts. Instead, we offer a wide range of self-help programs that enable people to find solutions to their own problems.

CAP works with people of all ages, at all levels of poverty, without regard to race, religion, nationality, sex or handicap.

One of Appalachia's greatest challenges is undervalued education–which has been passed from one generation to the next. But attitudes are beginning to change now as a result of CAP's child development centers and educational programs.

Volunteers–young and old alike–play a major role in dealing with problems facing the people of Appalachia. Without them, CAP's programs would most certainly suffer damaging setbacks.

CAP's child development centers work toward major goals, including development of positive self images, a love and excitement for learning, and spiritual awareness.

Most Appalachian people are proud of their heritage and prefer to stay in the mountains if they can find jobs to support themselves and their families.

was not very clean. Her bathroom was a metal bucket she emptied once or twice a day—usually at night so no one would see.

She had various ailments and needed to see a doctor frequently. She had arranged to get rides to the doctor's office from a young woman who lived down the road a bit, but when gasoline prices skyrocketed that fall, the woman wanted more money for the service than Emily could afford so the arrangement had ended. Now she had no way to get the medical care she needed.

Her husband had died years before, and she had no relatives in the state. She was literally alone in the world.

I looked around at Emily's home and her life and realized that more than anything else, Emily needed a friend.

Emily isn't alone in that need. We all rely on friends.

A friend is someone who drops everything to help you when you're in need. A friend is someone who always stops to talk, even, as Robert Frost says, when there are many hills to hoe.

I consider it a great honor to be a friend. Sure it brings responsibilities. There are times when it's not easy to be a friend. But the payoff is far greater than any inconvenience. That's why when Judy asked me if there was anything we could do for Emily—even though the CAP programs that could normally have helped Emily had run out of money—I said I'd think about it and pray. God would help me find a way.

As we drove home in the car it suddenly dawned on me that just days before, a doctor from Northern Kentucky had written to tell me that he had a mobile home trailer, 12 feet by 60 feet, that he no longer needed. He wrote that if I paid to move it, we could have it free.

The next week I drove North and examined the trailer. It was in good condition and would suit Emily's modest needs quite well. It was already wired and had a small bathroom. It could easily be hooked up to provide Emily with the lights, heat and indoor plumbing she so desperately needed. It would keep her warm and dry.

A few weeks later we had the trailer moved and installed on Emily's lot. As we finished the work Emily turned to me and said, "It sure is good to have a friend!"

I had planned to give the trailer to two nuns who worked for me. It would have saved me some money. But the sisters could live without the trailer—Emily couldn't. Sure, it cost $1,500 to transport, set up and get utilities to the trailer, but friendship is never cheap.

Elderly people like Emily are so much in need of friends here in Appalachia. Facing poverty and isolation, raised to believe in self-sufficiency, they will often suffer a great deal in silence rather than reach out to ask for help. That's why it's so important that we reach out to them.

There is a man around here they call Whacker. When I heard his story I felt great kinship to him. Eighteen years ago Whacker was involved in a deadly accident with a coal truck. The truck barreled down a steep incline and ran a stop light. It crossed the intersection and hit Whacker's car, killing his sister and two nieces. Whacker's back was broken, his knee was shattered and his skull was crushed. He survived, but just barely. Today he has a plate in his head, his back continues to give him serious trouble, and his shattered knee just barely bends.

Whacker is not the type to dwell on the past. For years he worked for the gas company and did the best he could. When he was laid off he survived working odd jobs. A few years ago he felt an irresistible urge to go home to the holler where he was raised. When he talks about the feeling that he had to go home, his eyes glisten with suppressed tears and his voice cracks.

"If I was going to be poor, I figured I might as well be poor at home."

For a while Whacker rented a tiny cabin while he tried to build himself a home on a piece of land near where his parents once lived.

To get to Whacker's place you have to climb a steep dirt path barely wide enough for a horse. You know you are near his house when you start tripping over his chickens. They scurry noisily along the road as you pass.

When you see Whacker's house you wonder why he feels such spiritual reverence for it. It's tiny, one story about 15 feet by 25 feet, just three rooms and a porch.

Whacker built most of it with his bare hands. How he saved enough money to buy the materials while working odd jobs I'll never know. He got all the way to the walls and the roof before his money and his luck ran out. His wife Gladys developed serious medical problems including diabetes and heart problems. Whacker himself has heart trouble and between the medical bills and the loss of work time Whacker just didn't have the money to put siding up or to sheetrock the interior walls of his little castle.

Without siding, of course, it was just a matter of time before the house rotted and crumbled and Whacker would be homeless again. When we put him on the list of CAP home repair projects, Whacker was "just tickled" that someone cared about his problems enough to help out.

Friends can surprise you like that.

When summer came we helped Whacker put up inexpensive masonite siding. It's not fancy but it keeps out the rain and protects the walls. We also helped him put up sheetrock interior walls so he could paint and finish the inside rooms.

Our garden seed program also provides Whacker and Gladys with seeds to plant a garden in the summer. Between the garden and the chickens and the four pigs Whacker raises, they can produce a large part of the food they need by themselves. That means a lot to Whacker.

Most recently, we helped Whacker when the gas company shut off his gas. The gas company was putting in a new line and charging the users a percentage of the installation costs. After paying medical bills and prescription expenses, Whacker and Gladys simply couldn't find the money, and the gas company—the same one that Whacker worked so hard for all those years—shut him off. We loaned him the money to get reconnected.

One of the things that is true about friends everywhere, but especially here among the people of these mountains, is that friends don't forget a favor. I know Whacker would do anything in his power to repay CAP for the friendship we've shown him. Someday we'll need some help in his neck of the woods and Whacker will be there, and he'll drop whatever he's doing to help us.

That's the promise friends give to each other.

The people of Appalachia don't forget the kindnesses of a friend. I remember an elderly woman named Mattie who had been befriended by a young CAP volunteer. David was a very special young man who managed to overcome the fear and suspicion that this woman, like many elderly women, had about young people and young men in particular. He had visited Mattie over many months to help ease her loneliness and make sure she was getting on okay.

Eventually his time as a volunteer was up but Mattie told me David was always on her mind and the friendship he gave her brightened many lonely days long after he had said goodbye.

She told me she had just received a wedding invitation from David and was absolutely astounded that he remembered her and that he had included her in this special occasion in his life. She couldn't travel to the wedding, but I know the pleasure of receiving the invitation from a friend a thousand miles away will live in her heart for the rest of her days.

So many of the elderly people we help feel that way about the people who support CAP financially. They are true friends no matter how far away they live. "Don't forget to thank them folks for me," they often remind me.

These promises of friends, both near and far, do remarkable things to a lonely elderly person. They ease the everyday burdens of living. They brighten the gloom and despair of poverty.

They make life worth living.

One of my favorite things is to visit our elderly homes and local nursing homes with a group of young toddlers from our child development centers. It's so wonderful to see the love of Christ flow from the children to the seniors and back again. No one gives love or friendship more freely than these little children, and no one needs it more than the elderly.

It is not only the elderly in Appalachia who need to feel they are part of a family. I remember an 89 year-old woman who wanted to come and volunteer with CAP. She wrote to me and then came to visit with her children. Her children, themselves in their sixties, were very apprehensive about her ability to work at her age.

After talking with her I told her to go home and pray about it. I was sure God would lead her to the right answer. I could see that she wanted very much to give her remaining years to God, but I wasn't too sure she was up to the task.

She went home and prayed and called to tell me that God had told her to stay home and reach out to His children by offering up her pain and suffering for the people of Appalachia.

Thousands of elderly people like her sacrifice and pray every day to be a friend and a part of our CAP family. Here are two letters I've received in recent weeks:

Dear Father Beiting:

You are a youngster compared to us. Art is 80 and I'm 76. We live on a very limited income but we have been blessed by God with good health and our ills have been minor. Thanks for your prayers. We sure do need them, and we pray for you and your projects every day.

Sincerely,
Art and Janet

Dear Father Beiting:

Your letter came the same day I mailed you my Christmas donation. I do want to send at least a little to help your work all the time. I don't have a lot, I'm a railroad pensioner, 84 years old, and I must manage carefully. I will pray for your work and help when I can.

Sincerely Yours,
Elizabeth

A few months ago I received a letter from an elderly gentleman who believed very strongly in our work. In fact, he told me he was putting off buying his medicine so he could send us a gift.

I wrote back to him and told him he shouldn't put off buying his medicine if doing so endangered his health . . . but I truly appreciate his sacrifice as proof of true friendship.

Another group that sorely needs our friendship in Appalachia is the handicapped. I don't know why we have so many handicapped people here. It may be due to poor nutrition and health care. Poor prenatal care and drug and alcohol abuse by expectant mothers probably increases the number of birth defects. Whatever the reason, we have an unusually high number of people with physical and developmental disabilities.

That's one reason why we started CAPrice Industries to offer direct employment to disabled adults in a sheltered workshop. But since we can't possibly hire every disabled person, we also concentrate on training the disabled for jobs in local businesses. In one of our most successful programs, we send a counselor out to an employer's site to learn a specific job. Once the counselor has mastered it, he or she teaches a disabled person the ropes and coaches them through the first few weeks at work.

Employers love the program because they get well-trained, dependable workers, and disabled people love it because it helps them build confidence before they go off on their own.

It's tough enough to find a job in Appalachia if you aren't disabled. Before CAPrice, the disabled didn't have much of a chance. I want to expand this effort until we can help find good, fulfilling jobs for all the handicapped people who need them.

A while ago a friend called to ask my advice about a program she was running. The program was funded by the state and provided job training for the disabled. The problem was that even after people were trained there was no one to hire them.

I assured her CAP would do everything it could. I vowed personally to do everything I could as well, so I hired a young man from her program

named David. I hoped he could help out around
the parish church. CAP is not a part of the Catholic Church and I run my parishes completely sep-
arate from my responsibilities to CAP, but I
wanted to get the ball rolling and provide an example.

David is 27 and mentally retarded. He was
trained to rake leaves and cut grass and do yard
work. He is a tireless worker and very good at
those tasks. He has worked for me now for six or
seven months and he has slowly but surely learned
to move onto other tasks like washing windows
and cleaning. I'm determined to teach him even
more so that we'll always have work for him to do.
He is enthusiastic about learning new things even
though it's very difficult for him.

As friends, David and I don't talk much. David
doesn't have much to say. He saves me a lot of
backbreaking work in my old age, and the look on
David's face when I tell him he's done a good job
and the satisfaction he gets from earning his pay
tells me that David appreciates our friendship
more deeply than almost any other friend I have.

I know we'll be good friends, helping each other
for as long as I live and he wants to stay.

One of the wonderful things about friendship is
that often it's so easy for one friend to help solve a
problem that seemed impossible to the other. It's
often very easy for our volunteers, backed up by
the generosity of our supporters, to offer the small

favors that can change a life.

Ruth's list of misfortunes could fill a larger book than this one. Just to name a handful, she is legally deaf, has severe asthma, a nervous disorder and serious dental problems. Her husband also has various health problems and can work only infrequently. Ruth has three children, one of whom also has hearing problems.

In spite of all this, Ruth is a very dedicated mother. Her youngest child is in one of our child development centers, and Ruth works diligently and faithfully in the center to help pay for her child's early start on education. She comes to all our parent meetings and parenting classes.

One day Ruth showed up for class with no teeth. A lovely young woman of 30, she looked 50 without her teeth. It turned out her dentist had insisted on pulling all her teeth to solve her worsening dental problems.

A few weeks went by and still Ruth didn't have any teeth. Finally, one of the teachers at the center asked Ruth when she'd be getting false teeth. Ruth said she had no idea because she didn't have the money.

As friends we couldn't let Ruth go on living without teeth so we found the money in one of our programs. We knew Ruth wanted to pay us back for the dentures so we worked out a way for her to pay us a little at a time. The next time Ruth showed up to work at the center she wore a bright, beautiful smile that was partly the result of her new teeth, but mostly the result of the glow of friendship she reflected.

The most remarkable thing about this kind of loving friendship to the people of Appalachia is that it is almost always repaid. Maybe not in dollars and cents, but it does get repaid.

A year ago I met a family who lived on the Tug Fork River. Marlene and Bill were very poor. They had both lost their jobs and they had three children to support. Their children were struggling in the local schools so I arranged for them to attend the Catholic private school in the area even though they aren't Catholic, and they couldn't pay for it. I'd call them whenever there were odd jobs that needed to be done and I paid them as generously as I could. At Christmas time last year, I took up a collection in my own family to get toys and food so that they could have a real celebration of Jesus' birth.

I tried very hard to be a good friend to them — I hope I succeeded.

This past summer Bill found a job in Indiana, and the family moved away. I was very happy for them that they'd found work but I was saddened that I'd lost some good friends and that yet one more family had to flee Appalachia to find work.

On Thanksgiving Day I was very busy. I had to cover religious services in three counties and by the time I got home, I was dead tired. I was also lonely, feeling the regrets that always hit me during the holidays when I imagine families sharing their love around a dinner table. Finally, in the early evening, I decided to just go to sleep and hope my loneliness passed.

Just before I dozed off the phone rang. It was Marlene. She said they were offering thanks at the dinner table and they realized how many of the things they had to be thankful for that year came about because of my friendship. She was calling to thank me. I spent half an hour on the phone with them, catching up on their lives and talking with the children.

When I finally hung up I was rejuvenated and the feelings of loneliness were gone. As far as I'm concerned, any favors I ever did for them were repaid in full by that one phone call that shattered my loneliness and made me feel loved.

Nearly 40 years ago I met a man named Jim. A neighbor of his asked me to go and see if Jim needed help. When I sat down with Jim, he told me that his wife was dying of cancer, and he had five little girls to care for.

I didn't have the resources to help in a big way, and Jim never asked for anything more than friendship, so that's what I gave them. I visited as often as I could and brought small gifts like used clothing or toys for the girls.

About six months after I met them, Jim's wife died and the family moved away. I didn't hear from Jim again until this letter came last month:

Dear Father Beiting,
 I hope you have fully recovered from that awful car wreck. I will never forget you for the friendship you showed us when my wife was dying of cancer. We had thought we were all alone. I didn't have any family nearby and neither did my wife. I belonged to a Masonic Lodge at the time, but they never came by to visit.
 You were the only one who was there for us.
 All these years I have wanted to pay you back but my ship hadn't come in. Now it has, and I am enclosing a check for CAP. I hope it can change darkness to light for someone else, just as you brought light to our lives forty years ago.

Best Wishes,
Jim

 I don't know when I've received a letter I have treasured so much. All I had ever done for Jim was be a friend. I couldn't save his wife's life. I couldn't erase his financial problems or help him raise his five little girls. All I did was say, "You are not alone."
 That's all it took to help him go on.
 You can't weigh friendship on a scale nor record it on a ledger sheet. If you looked at reports of what CAP does every year, things like distributing seeds to nearly 7,500 people, sheltering more than

1,000 women and children in family abuse centers, serving more than 36,000 troubled people in need, you'd never get the slightest impression of what CAP is really about. CAP is really about children of God meeting one to one to share their lives.

Jesus said the greatest commandment was to love your God with all your heart. He said the second was like the first, "Love your neighbor as yourself." I think it's very interesting that He said the second is very much like the first. They don't seem that similar at first glance.

But if we remember that God lives in every tired, lonely old woman shivering in an isolated shack, every elderly couple struggling to keep their lives together in the face of poverty, every disabled and disadvantaged person—in fact in every person—we can see why Jesus said the second commandment was the same as the first.

If you really want to love God, you will find Him right beside you in your neighbor.

At another time Jesus described the day of retribution in heaven. He said God will put the sheep on His right and the goats on His left. He will say to those on His right: "Come, you blessed of my father, inherit the kingdom prepared for you. When I was hungry you gave Me to eat. When I was thirsty you gave Me to drink. When I was a stranger you took Me in. When I was naked you clothed Me. When I was sick you visited Me and when I was in prison you came to Me."

When the righteous ask the Lord when did they ever do these things, He will answer, "Truly I say to you, whenever you did these things for the least of My brothers, you did them for Me."

Jesus promised that those sheep would have eternal life with their Father in heaven — not a bad promise from the greatest friend of all.

A while back we had a party for some of the younger children in our child development centers. When the party was over and I was getting ready to leave, one of the parents of the children stopped me to talk. As I chatted with the parent, I overheard her two boys whispering. One of them said, "Do you know who that man is?"

The other one answered, "Yeah, I know him, he goes to my church. He's my friend."

I could never receive a greater compliment. There is no greater title on this earth than "Friend" . . . not priest, not president, not even king. No one who has ever been a friend, whether to the family next door, or to families in Appalachia, should ever lose sight of the tremendous accomplishment that title signifies nor of the great responsibilities it carries. The promises of a friend are the ties that bind us together — they should never be broken.

The Promise of Independence

My brother did the climbing; and at first
Threw me down grapes to miss and scatter
And have to hunt for in sweet fern and hardhack;
Which gave him some time to himself to eat,
But not so much, perhaps, as a boy needed.
So then, to make me wholly self-supporting,
He climbed still higher and bent the tree to earth
And put it in my hands to pick my own grapes.

Robert Frost, from *Wild Grapes*

"If people do for me then I'll be 'done for'," Barbara said as I sat on her front porch.

"I want to do for myself," she insisted.

Barbara is trying with all her heart and soul to raise her son Nathan by herself. She faces a daunting task with the determination I see so often in the people of Appalachia.

Nathan was born with microcephaly, cerebral palsy, seizure disorders and mental retardation. Barbara's daily routine with Nathan includes speech therapy, occupational therapy, physical therapy, medication schedules and educational sessions. She is driven to give him the chance to make the most of his life. She wants him to have the same independence she cherishes so deeply.

"I pray that Nathan gets everything he needs, but I don't want someone else to give it to him. I want to do it myself. That's why I'm glad CAP's special education teachers don't do everything for me. I want them to show me how to do it."

The people of Appalachia have a special tie to the promise of independence. Isolated from the rest of America in the frontier days, we learned to make everything we needed with our own hands. What we couldn't make we did without. We neither got nor asked for help from the outside world.

That heritage runs deep in the blood here, but in the last fifty years it has been sorely tested. Welfare programs have their place, and I could never deny that they have saved countless families from absolute starvation. But they have also eroded the tradition of self-sufficiency and independence that defines the Appalachian spirit.

That's why I have always insisted that CAP give people a helping hand—not a permanent handout. Many times volunteers have said to me, "They have no money for food or clothes or heat. Why don't we just give them the money?"

When I look at the desperate needs I too am tempted. It would be so easy to spend our resources to just give people what they don't have. That would be the easy way. But every time we give something to them we'll take something far more valuable away—the promise of independence, of freedom. What we need to do is bend the tree to earth, as in Robert Frost's poem, and let the Appalachian people pick their own grapes.

When we think of slavery we think of overlords and dictators. But it's just as easy—and just as crushing—to become a slave to a welfare agency, a volunteer, or even an old white-haired missionary priest like me.

God didn't make us to be slaves to either camp.

God understands the human soul far better than we. He knows we take no pride and gain no satisfaction in what we're told to do or in what's done for us—only in what we do ourselves. That's why He has always left the final steps in our salvation up to us. The independence and freedom He has given us is a great gift. It is also a great burden, but it's the only way we ever gain anything we can truly call our own, whether it's salvation or an education or a job.

After 42 years in the mountains, watching dozens of "give-away" programs come and go—in failure—I am more than ever convinced that the path on which we set out long ago was right.

The other day I met a woman who reinforced that conviction. The local hospital called to say a patient wanted to see me. When I got there I was introduced to Susan, a woman in her fifties. Susan had an enlarged liver, a growth on her stomach and a number of other ailments. As I talked with her I became more and more impressed by her courage and determination.

She had six children. Her husband left her when she was pregnant with the sixth. She never heard from him again and never received a penny in child support. Susan cleaned houses, did yard work — whatever she could to support her growing children. For twenty years she gave up every waking minute of her life for those children.

Now that all her children are grown and living their own lives, Susan has gone back to school to become a teacher. When I met with her at the hospital, Susan was upset that she might miss the rest of the semester's work. She asked me if I could call the director of the college and work out a way for her to continue to study, or to make up the work when she was feeling better.

Two days later I went back to visit her again to report on my conversation with the director. When I got there I found out Susan had new problems. Her youngest daughter, only recently married, had been told that she had cancer — and that she was pregnant. On top of that, the young woman's husband had just recently lost his job and could not find another one. Because they were so strapped for money, Susan gave them the money she had saved for her next semester's tuition.

Finally, Susan's doctor had told her that same morning that he was afraid she might have liver cancer.

Through this tale of unending woe, Susan never once asked for help. She was determined to solve these problems within her own family. I think she sensed that taking the easy way out would rob her of the wonderful feeling that comes from triumphing over adversity.

That's a reward Susan has come to love.

Even though she didn't ask, we did try to help a little. We found some baby clothes in the boxes of rummage clothes donated to us. I was able to find a few part time jobs that Susan's son-in-law could do to earn some money.

Mostly, I gave Susan moral support and told her she was on the right track. I think that's what she really wanted and needed.

This family has a long way to go. As I write this, Susan's health and the health of her daughter are unsure. But I am betting that they will survive and that in a couple of years Susan will graduate from college. I hope she invites me because I'd be honored to share in her personal triumph of independence.

Independence is too valuable a right and too great a need for us to squander no matter how noble our goals. I tell our volunteers and workers that the real need is not the food, the shelter, or the clothes. The real need is the sense of dignity and self-worth found in true independence and freedom. The real act of charity is to help people regain their independence. That's the real promise we have to keep.

"We are not giving, we are investing in the future," I remind them.

It's not an easy lesson to learn. I learned it myself long ago on that dark road when I realized how futile were my efforts to "give away" food and clothes. Today we use the gifts of our donors and our volunteers to help families get started down the road to independence. We use our resources to encourage and provide coaching and education. We teach people the skills and ideas they can use to build their own lives of hope.

Barbara (Nathan's mother) is on the way, and we are right there beside her—not behind her pushing and not in front of her pulling, but beside her, lending a helping hand until she learns what she needs from us and can continue on her own.

Each spring we bring her seeds through our garden seed program. We don't plant them for her. We show her how to plant them and how to harvest and preserve her crop. We tutor her in her quest to gain a high school equivalency certificate. Hopefully she will pass the test this spring.

Barbara loves her independence and wants the same for Nathan. She dreams of the day "Nathan will be able to do for hisself."

"I don't care if he ain't got it in him to do nothin' more than he does today—but if it is in him—well he's gonna get a chance."

It has taken a long time for Appalachia to slip from independence into the slavery of poverty and reliance on welfare programs. It will take a long time for Appalachia to escape and be free again. But each small step along the way is cause for celebration.

Nathan took one of those small steps last fall. Through a donor's gift, we provided Nathan with a tape recorder and some telephone answering machine cassettes. Another parent of a special needs child rigged a special switch so that with a little effort Nathan can reach out and activate the words, "Mom, could you please come here?"

"I don't have to be wondering if he's okay all the time," Barbara smiled, "and most of all, it's something he does for hisself. I may have to do a lot for him when I get there, but Nathan does his own callin'. I'd say that's a good start!"

It IS a good start. Soon Nathan will be ready for a more complicated communication board. His independence has begun.

So has Barbara's. And so will Appalachia's. With each new step of independence Appalachia grows stronger, more resilient and more resourceful. When I contemplate my own mortality, my only prayer is that I live long enough to see that glorious day when the promise of independence comes true.

The Promise of Hard Work

And nothing to look backward to with pride,
And nothing to look forward to with hope,
So now and never any different.

Robert Frost, from *The Death of the Hired Hand*

In America we have always banked on the promise of hard work. The idea of a fair wage for a full day's work runs deep in our national soul. In fact, this "work ethic" is one of the secrets of our success among nations.

We tell our children, "You can be anything you want to if you put your mind to it and work!"

That promise of hard work rings very hollow in Appalachia today.

In past years the coal industry provided jobs for almost anyone who wanted to work in this area. It was backbreaking, dirty, dangerous work but you could earn a living and support a family if you were willing to sweat. The industry attracted thousands of people from all over the country to come and settle here.

The coal industry is no longer the employment force it once was. The industry is increasingly mechanized, so each year fewer and fewer people can earn a living working for coal companies.

Unfortunately, nothing has yet risen to replace the jobs lost to coal.

The loss to Appalachia's people goes far—far beyond the loss of income. Being out of work drains the life from people, disrupts families, and leaves them feeling worthless and wasted.

The loss of coal jobs has also caused the failure of many related industries. Around Christmas time last year, I met a family that had fallen on hard times. Ed, the father and husband of the family, had been a builder for many years. Now his health was bad and since so few people build houses anymore in this part of Appalachia, his contracting business had failed. He had three teen-age children to raise and he couldn't find a job.

When I heard about his plight I was trying to figure out how to get the attic of one of my churches insulated. The church is a house with a simple tin roof. It cost a fortune to heat. I offered to pay Ed to put up insulation and sheetrock in the attic.

The look on Ed's face when he picked up his first paycheck would explain what I'm saying far better than I ever could. Ed hated the thought of applying for welfare or food stamps. To be able to do a useful job and earn money to support his family restored his pride. There was a bounce in his step and he held his head a little higher when he went home that first payday.

As citizens of the United States many of Appalachia's poorest people receive welfare and food stamps and assistance from programs like that. I guess these programs have their value if they keep families from starving to death, but to me they are a razor-sharp double-edged sword.

They may keep families alive in body, but they destroy their souls. Human beings are not meant to be idle—we were meant to work. Welfare takes away the incentive to work. It also takes away the rewards of work. I don't blame families who have no other way to feed their children but I see the damage that is done every single day; I see their will sapped and their self-esteem sink lower and lower and lower.

Walter was always a hard working man who worked for the forestry department for years. He can instantly identify every tree that grows in these hills—and there are dozens of species. He was laid off a while ago, and now he has no work. It's killing him.

Anyone who imagines that being on welfare is a breeze or who envies the fact that Walter doesn't work anymore is crazy. Just ask all the people who retire and then find out that not working depresses them and drives them crazy—and those people are mostly over 65. Imagine not working when you are 50 or 40 . . . or 20.

People are meant to work. I mentioned before

that I always say that "tired volunteers are happy volunteers." It works the same way with all people. We are happiest when we are busy, accomplishing things of real value.

There aren't enough tired—or happy—people in Appalachia these days.

I wish I could say that people like Ed and Walter are exceptions but they aren't. This area has one of the highest unemployment rates in the country and has had that distinction for nearly thirty years. Through economic booms and recessions we still keep suffering.

I was raised in the Great Depression and I vividly remember the despair and hopelessness on the faces of the scores and scores of unemployed men. I remember my father working three jobs and still having to beg and borrow food from my aunt. I hope and pray that America never sees that kind of suffering again.

Unfortunately, Appalachia has been in a nearly continuous "Great Depression" for decades.

Beyond simple unemployment, we also suffer from underemployment and unfair wages.

As I was driving a few weeks ago I saw a young man of about 25 or so hitchhiking and stopped to pick him up. We got to talking and he told me that he was on his way to pick up his paycheck. I was glad to hear he had a job so I asked him what he did.

He told me he was a stock clerk in a supermarket. Not exactly a high paying job but everyone has to start somewhere, I thought.

"Are you off work today?" I asked him.

"Yeah, I only work 30 hours a week."

"How come you don't work full time?"

"I'd love to work full time," he said, "but they won't let me. If I work 40 hours a week they'd have to give me health benefits. So instead they limit my hours and hire more part-time people so they don't have to pay anyone health benefits."

This kind of manipulation of employees strikes me as breaking the promise of hard work.

Appalachia wants to work and work hard. The people here carved their lives out of the wilderness and out of the stone beneath these mountains. Theirs is not a slothful heritage. Hard work is in their bones and in their blood.

It kills them to be thought of as "living off the crumbs thrown to them by the rest of America." They want to pull their own weight and hold their heads up high.

That's why CAP is doing everything we can to bring jobs to Appalachia. We try to provide examples to get people thinking and restore their confidence.

For several years a generous office of AT&T in New Jersey has been sending CAP their used office furniture which we store and distribute to our own offices and to the many organizations and churches that need furniture for their operations.

One day I was in the warehouse where we keep the furniture, and I noticed a pile off to one side. When I asked about it, I was told that those pieces were so badly ripped or broken that we couldn't give them to anyone.

I immediately thought of a man I knew who was struggling to make some extra money by reupholstering furniture in his back yard. I phoned him and several other people who also did that kind of work and asked if they'd be interested in repairing this used furniture. They agreed and we created three new jobs in an afternoon.

I wish the generous people in New Jersey could see the pride these men take in their work and what it means to their families. The look on a little boy's face when he shows me the chair his pappy fixed says it all. I'm half tempted to tear some seat covers on purpose just to create more jobs.

But CAP can't possibly create enough jobs to save Appalachia alone. There must be two parts to the solution.

First, existing businesses must be enticed to relocate here, and we need to start new industries centered in Appalachia.

I don't yet know how we'll do this. I pray every day for God's guidance and I ask anyone in America who has an idea to write to me. Until then we'll keep doing the best we can to convince companies to come here, one business at a time.

The second part of the answer is education for

Appalachia's adults. Our adult illiteracy rate is one of the highest in the nation and is a severe handicap to our economic growth.

When we put these two parts together we will re-create the promise of hard work here in Appalachia.

All through the Bible there are references to the value of work, and Jesus' own mission was often described as His "works." I think God knows how much of people's self-worth comes from the work they do and how much they suffer when they have no work.

As I said, CAP can't rebuild Appalachia's economy and the promise of hard work alone, but we're not afraid nor ashamed to take small steps that help a family here and a family there. If we could all do a small part I know that the promise can be fulfilled and Appalachia can get back to work again. If we don't, then we have, as Robert Frost said, "nothing to look backward to with pride, and nothing to look forward to with hope, so now and never any different."

I promise I won't let that be our future.

An Education of Promise

A tree's leaves may be ever so good,
So may its bark, so may its wood;
But unless you put the right thing to its root
It will never show much flower or fruit.

Robert Frost, from *Leaves Compared With Flowers*

Just recently I attended a talk given by the former Director of Human Resources for the state of Kentucky. He pointed out in his address that if you eliminated the 5th and 7th congressional districts, which are the mountain areas where CAP's work is focused, Kentucky would rank among the most well-educated states in the nation. As it is we rank among the least well-educated.

I think this shows how serious our education problem is in the Appalachian regions of Kentucky and other states. In some of the counties we serve, more than half the people do not have an eighth grade education. Over 400,000 Kentuckians are functionally illiterate.

Of all of the strikes against renewal in this poverty-stricken area, the lack of education is the greatest. I compare the people of Appalachia to the plants in the Robert Frost poem. No matter how much native intelligence and ingenuity the people have—and they have a great deal—without education they will never show flower, nor bear fruit. They will never be able to leap the hurdles they face to take their proper place in American society.

Education opens doors to jobs and opportunity. It leads to a greater understanding of our nation, our world, and our God. It promises to change the future for Appalachia.

Reversing a century of poor education in the mountains is a daunting task. This summer while I was sitting at a campfire at one of our summer camps, I struck up a conversation with a young boy.

I asked him about his dreams for the future and how he was working towards them in school.

"School's a pain," he said, "It ain't worth nuthin'."

"What do you mean?" I pressed him.

"Man, I have to walk a mile to my bus stop everyday, in the rain and stuff, and sit through all day, and then walk all the way home again.

"I'd rather stay home and work with my old man doing carpentry."

I tried to tell him that if he got an education he could do anything. He could still work with his father if he wanted, but he'd be better at it. And maybe he'd decide to go on to something else. I told him that education by itself was valuable. It opened the mind and the soul and was a pathway to the whole world.

"My old man can't even read and he gets by. He says school is for mama's boys," was his response.

I was depressed for a week about him and his chances of succeeding in this world with that attitude learned at his father's knee. Unfortunately, his attitude is not unique. So many parents are illiterate and so embarrassed and defensive about their illiteracy that they will make fun of school and learning rather than look bad in front of their children.

It's a feeling I can certainly understand, but I wish they could see that there's another way. I believe that to truly bring about a revolution in education in Appalachia we must teach both the parents and the children.

Last summer I attended a celebration for a class of our adult students who had just taken and passed their high school equivalency tests. We organize the celebration in the same fashion as a graduation so that the "graduates" get a strong feeling of the importance of their achievement.

At this particular graduation a woman stood up and spoke out to the group.

"I dropped out of school in grade school. I didn't think it was worth it. My mother couldn't read, and my father couldn't read, and I didn't see any use in it.

"I'm sorry to say that my own kids did the same thing. But now I see how wrong I was and I have never been prouder than I am right now. I have three grandchildren, and I'm determined to make sure they don't make the same mistake. I talk to them all the time about school, and I give them little prizes and presents whenever they do well.

"And now I'm going to work on my children. I told them, 'I failed you once. I'm not going to fail you again.' If it's the last thing I do, I'm going to convince them all to get their high school equivalency certificates, too."

When she sat down the audience gave her a standing ovation that lasted several minutes.

I was tremendously excited. This was a real start. By helping one woman, we had started a chain reaction that was going to bring new hope to an entire family. With this kind of hope we could change Appalachia forever.

That's why I am so enthusiastic about our School on Wheels program. There are many adults who can't or won't attend a regular classroom. They want to learn and want to grow but because of their age and their embarrassment about their lack of ability to read or write they can't bring themselves to "go to school."

We bring the school to them. We train local volunteers and give them transportation so they can go out in the valleys and hills to people's homes. The first time the tutor shows up, it's always awkward. The adult is often afraid to admit he or she can't read. It can be very difficult to admit that—especially to a younger person. That's why I wish we could get more older people and even senior citizens to come to Appalachia to volunteer to tutor.

After a few lessons the discomfort is usually gone, and the real education can begin. There is nothing more fulfilling than to start with a person who can't even read road signs and then realize that after a few months he or she can read a short book or start to read the newspaper. Once they get started most adults so quickly see the value of reading that they work very hard and progress rapidly.

And the pride on their faces when they receive a high school equivalency certificate is worth all the effort a hundred times over.

Of course, learning to read is not all there is to an education of promise. One of our greatest problems in Appalachia is that we are woefully short on family-life education. We don't know how to be good mothers and fathers and husbands and wives. In a well-functioning society, children learn their parenting and marriage skills from their own parents. For the last 50 years or so, many Appalachian children have learned only despair from their parents.

That's why we have organized parental support
groups and classes to retrain many of our young
parents. We start by reminding them that their
family is the most precious thing they'll ever have.
It should be the center of life and love. We teach
couples how to show their love for each other and
how to work out problems. We teach them how to
correct children without belittling them, and how
to love them without spoiling them. We encourage
them to foster learning and reward good achievement.

When a society is so steeped in poverty and
despair, these simple skills wither away. Parents
who are worried about how to put food on the
table find it terribly hard to find time to love each
other and to teach and encourage their children
the way they should. Parents who are lost to the
evil of alcohol abuse often lose all control of their
actions, and beat and emotionally torture the ones
they love most in the world.

Appalachian parents are not short on love.
Family ties are very strong here. We must try to
rechannel that love in the right direction.

What may be the most promising education is a
spiritual education. Jesus said, "Man shall not live
on bread alone, but on every word that comes
from the mouth of God."

Throughout our educational programs for both
children and adults we keep this foremost in our
minds. That's why I consider our Bible schools to

be every bit as important as our regular classrooms. Even in our regular classrooms and adult-
education programs, we mix inter-denominational
Christian witness in with reading and writing and
algebra. There is nothing more important than
learning about the God who saves us and who is
our only hope for Appalachia.

Our belief that education must be more than
reading, writing and arithmetic sometimes puts us
at odds with the educational establishment. That
doesn't bother me. I think CAP has to be a friendly rebel at times. We have to challenge the party
line. Sometimes we have to stand up and say that
education that only prepares people to work is not
enough because getting a job and earning money is
not enough. It's an old saying, but true, that
money can't buy happiness.

Happiness comes with doing God's will. It is far
more important that we love than that we earn.

Strange as it sounds, our society is filled with
emptiness. We have tried materialism and secular-
ism and we have bled our souls dry in the process.

That's why, in our educational programs, we
stress the deeper values of life and religion. When
you've learned to feel and respond to the hurt of a
neighbor, learned to sacrifice, learned the lasting
value of friendship—and most importantly, learned to listen to God with your heart—then you
have an education that prepares you to love. Add
to that a little reading, writing and arithmetic and

nothing could ever hold you back.

This is the education of promise we bring to the youth and the little children.

When I see people like the grandmother who stood up at our high school equivalency graduation I am very optimistic. Lack of education is our greatest liability, but it provides our greatest hope. I have a vision of Appalachia fifty years from now. Some people would say it's a crazy vision, but I don't think so.

Since finding good locations for heavy industries like manufacturing is so hard here in these steep mountains and valleys, I see a future where Appalachia becomes a center of education and higher learning. We could use the exceptional beauty of this land as a lure to attract high-tech industry that thrives in areas with a highly educated populace. We could become an international, intellectual and technological force.

I'll admit, it's a crazy dream . . . but not an impossible one . . . not if we start now and if we trust in God to help us.

Carol, one of our volunteers, told me how she helped a woman named Brandy get enrolled at a local college. Brandy is forty years old, well past the normal college age. Carol drove Brandy to the college to help her move into an apartment with her two children.

When Carol walked out of the college registration office with Brandy she was surprised to see

Brandy crying. "What's the matter?" she asked.

Brandy's reply was enlightening, "I'm just standing here picturing myself on my graduation day and I am so happy I have to cry."

Brandy has a long way to go in her personal search for an education of promise but just the vision of the future is enough to make her cry tears of joy.

I feel the same way about the educational future of Appalachia. In my prayers every day I have promised God and the people of Appalachia that I will do my part.

The Promise of the Future

The woods are lovely, dark, and deep,
But I have promises to keep,
And miles to go before I sleep,
And miles to go before I sleep.

Robert Frost, from *Stopping by Woods on a
Snowy Evening*

A while ago I received a letter from a woman who lives here in Appalachia.

Dear Father Beiting,

I was born and reared here in Harlan County. I attended our local schools and then went on to the University of Kentucky to receive a teaching degree.

This is my 13th year of teaching. I'm now 39 years old, and I must be getting jaded because what I see here now makes me want to give up.

I see families who have always depended on government assistance and have come to expect it as their God-given right. I see children with bright minds who are throwing their lives and their futures away because in their families it's an embarrassment to do well in school.

On the opposite side of the coin I see older citizens who have always tried to improve their communities. They won't live forever and I worry that we're headed for an even bleaker future.

Since you've been in our region longer than I have, I am dying to know your philosophy. How do you keep from giving up? What are the answers and have you seen any improvement? Can you give me hope of change? Can you give me hope, period?

Thanks for listening,
Shirley

I'd be a liar if I denied that some of these same thoughts have come into my head from time to time. But a few days after I received Shirley's letter I received another letter that answered her question better than I could.

Dear Father Beiting,

Something happened the other day that reminded me of a lesson you taught me when I volunteered for you in 1967.

During a homily at daily Mass you talked about what you called secondary service—the small unglamorous tasks that enable the more visible ministry to go on and that enable the good we do to go beyond us in ways we can't predict.

The other day my husband helped a black

woman get her stalled car started. The woman said it was the first human kindness she had ever been shown by a white person. I met her again a few days after that, and she told me that later that day she came upon another stranded motorist and stopped to help as a way of passing the favor on.

I wanted to tell you this story to remind you not to get discouraged if you can't do everything you once did. The winds of the spirit blow where they will, and the littlest things become great and go far beyond us when God takes them out of our hands. It takes faith to believe, without seeing, that God can make good come from what we no longer control.

Much love to you.

Love in Jesus,
Kathy

In this past year I have had great cause to ponder Kathy's reminder.

Before the accident last January, I had ambitious plans for the year. I was going to build more churches in my work as a priest. I was going to start new programs for the poor in my role as the leader of the Christian Appalachian Project. I was feeling indestructible and full of energy. I thought 1990 was going to be my year.

Well, I found out I wasn't indestructible. In an instant my life was transformed to one of hospitals and convalescent homes. I had to rely on doctors and nurses for daily instructions. I had to have people drive me where I wanted to go. I was confined to my bed for months.

I received a great and lasting lesson in humility. I found out I wasn't the center of the world — that it wasn't my strength and wisdom that were going to save the people of Appalachia.

In my early years in these mountains, I often imagined what I would do once poverty was defeated. At age 26 I couldn't imagine that any problem could outlast me. When this challenge was conquered, I planned to go to South America and take up a new challenge among the poor there.

Now, after 40 years, I see that the enemy is far greater than I ever suspected. The needs are greater, the despair is greater. I have come to accept the fact that I will not live to see the total victory I counted on when I was 26.

That too is a humbling thing for me.

But I can't accept Shirley's pessimism. I understand it completely, but I won't accept it.

In fact, I am more committed now than I have ever been. If I had known when I was 26 what I know now, I think I would have given up and moved on. Today my knowledge of the magnitude of the problem just makes me feel that the victory will be all that much greater when we get there.

Over the years I have also grown to understand that this will not be my victory . . . it will be God's. I hope I've played a part, but in the end it will be God who hears the cries of the poor and comes to the aid of His children.

The power to defeat the enemy we face is not in me. If it were, poverty would be over now, because I have continually given all I have. The power lies with God. When we have learned that and learned to call on Him and do His will then the victory will come.

These days I am constantly reminded of the scripture passage that was my favorite when I was a young man in the seminary. God says, "I am the vine, you are the branches. Life flows from the vine, the branches are lifeless without it."

While I have always loved that beautiful message I don't think I ever really understood it until this year. That's why I look more and more to God every day. I have decided my job is to endure, not passively but actively, by saying to God, "Thy will be done." If He wants my pain, my frustration, my defeats, He can have them. If He wants anything else from me, He can have it. In this surrender and acceptance of His will I have gained more courage than I ever had before.

I have also realized that I have to rely on others more than ever. I also realize that the Christian Appalachian Project and the people who support it are not a collection of individuals, but a family—a people of God.

On these ideas I have built new strength.

The other day a man came to me and told me

that I should give up on my idea to build a church in his town. "We're all too old for this," he said. "There's no real reason to make this kind of effort. Why don't we just be content and do what we can?"

I told him, "I was not commissioned to be a minister of God to preside at funerals. I want to be a herald of the Resurrection. I want to be a messenger that Jesus lives."

I love Appalachia. Not because I am especially good or generous but because this is a land with much to love. There are people and places here that inspire deep, lasting love.

But there are also people and places here that can break your heart. I can never forget the little children living in falling-down houses, wearing dirty rags, who will never learn to read. I can never forget the old man huddled alone by his potbellied stove in an old shed not fit for animals. I can never forget the old ladies who sit in tiny living rooms praying that someone will come by to talk to them and break the loneliness. I can never forget the shame felt by young parents who break their backs trying to support a family only to have to apply for food stamps, because everything they've done is still not enough.

We have to bring hope to these people. As children of God we are called and commanded to this task. We are not necessarily promised victory—at least not in our lifetimes. What is important is not the victory but the struggle itself. I may not live to see the complete victory. But if my span of time on earth is part of the answer, that's all that counts. If I am part of something good, what more could I ask for?

I hope all those people who volunteer for CAP and who support us so generously feel the same way. This is truly a noble effort. Maybe even more so because the end is not yet in sight.

It's easy to begin a marathon when you are well rested. It's easy to finish it when the end is in sight. The glory comes in between when it's a struggle to just keep moving.

We must also remember that while we haven't yet defeated poverty and despair and loneliness here in Appalachia, we have helped countless individuals and families. Some people would say that doesn't really matter because the society as a whole is still suffering. I say it does matter. Every time we change darkness to light it counts. If we can light enough candles and stop cursing the darkness we'll chase away the night.

Don't forget our God is a personal God. He didn't come to save humanity as a whole. He came to save each of us individually. Jesus said, "Are not five sparrows sold for two cents? And yet not one of them is forgotten before God. Indeed, the very hairs of your head are all numbered. Do not fear; you are of more value than many sparrows."

I know that God rejoices over every single act of

love towards His children. And I know that He will multiply those small acts of love until the valleys ring with laughter once more.

That will be a wonderful day.

I know it will come. When I witness the love and generosity of CAP's supporters and volunteers, I know it will come. When people tell me that greed and materialism run rampant in our nation, I always point out that selfless generosity also runs rampant. I show them letters from supporters who've sacrificed greatly just to help their brothers and sisters in Appalachia. I tell them about volunteers who've given up years of their lives to come here to work for a pittance.

There are promises to keep and hard work to be done here in Appalachia and so many good people want to be a part. That, Shirley, is the hope you look for. With good people beside us and God above us we cannot fail.

We have miles and miles to go before we sleep, but we do not walk those miles alone. If we lean on our friends and follow the direction God shows us, we will reach the end someday.

This is a good way to lead a life—following God, surrounded by such people. We should hold our heads up high, let the wind blow in our hair, let the sun shine on us by day and the stars by night. We know not where the road ends, but we are on the way. We are on the way—with promises to keep and miles to go before we sleep.

A Volunteer's Promise to Father Beiting

Father Beiting made very few promises to his volunteers. He promised we would go to bed tired. He promised that the greatest gift of our work would be what would happen to us through doing it. He promised that with God's help all things are possible.

We saw these promises realized every day, in hope, courage, faith and love. Father's daily example made our mission work come alive with God's spirit.

Our promises to him, on the other hand, were somewhat more numerous and complex.

We promised to pray.

Every morning we would get up at 7:20 AM, knock each other down the stairs and hop across the church lawn, putting on shoes and socks in transit. We would trip up the stairs, ease the front door open and utter our first prayer of thanksgiving that Father Beiting (already deep in prayer in the front pew) had not noticed our tardiness. Safely in our pious places, we would reel with shock and disdain at the unfortunate volunteer whose late arrival was announced by the squeaky left door (we always used the right).

Father's silver head would gently shake, his great shoulders would sigh and his eyes would gaze somewhere beyond the ceiling. Perhaps he was lifting up his eyes unto the hills from whence came his patience to deal with us.

Although our arrival lacked a certain polish and our morning hymns were somewhat off-key, the impact of those prayers shared and offered on those mornings is still very much a part of me. It was there that we found the soul of CAP. It was there that we renewed our sense of purpose and deepened our personal and community spirituality. And I promise you again, Father, to continue those prayers and to hopefully draw from them all my life.

We promised to be good stewards.

All of our work was done through the faith and support of others throughout the country. Our donors were very much a part of our work and prayers, and Father Beiting kept us continually aware of what a privilege and responsibility it is to be entrusted with someone else's generosity. Whether the donation was ten dollars from an elderly man who walked to his doctor's appointment and sent us his cab fare or a truckload of food and clothes, we learned to treasure each gift and see that it was put to good use.

I remember one year a generous company sent us sorghum. We must have received two or three trucks full of sorghum. When we had given away all we could, we still had too much — and Father instructed us that there would be no more maple syrup, honey or sugar until the sorghum was gone. We poured it on pancakes, waffles, toast and biscuits. We tried it in coffee, tea and oatmeal. We chilled it in the refrigerator and heated it on the stove. When the "Day of the Last Jar" arrived we were jubilant. As we were putting away the pots and pans of supper we discovered one-more-jar-of-sorghum. Without a moment's hesitation we took the jar quietly to the backyard and buried it. I expect it's still there.

With the exception of that momentary lapse in stewardship, I hope and pray that we have delivered each donor's gift with the spirit in which it was given. The transaction of a gift from a faith-filled giver to a faith-filled receiver is, in fact, the realization of the Kingdom of God on earth. As volunteers, we saw that faith justified with our own eyes.

I've watched my mother and father join thousands of others who carefully fold and pack clothing and food in church basements. I've stood in the warehouses, dwarfed by mountains of boxes filled with generosity and faith. I've greeted weary volunteer truck drivers whose droopy eyes smile as they admit their underestimation of the long haul through the mountains. I've sat with a young mother as she placed her infant in a donated crib with a prayer of thanksgiving that her baby had a clean, safe place to rest. The power of the transaction from giver-through-Christ to receiver is overwhelming. Beyond this I really don't have the words to describe it. But I can renew my promise to you, Father, to try to remember always what a humbling honor it is to be the steward of our donors' generosity.

One of our most common promises still raises a blush: "We promise, Father, we will never do that again!

"We promise never to put Jello in your good shoes again.

"We promise we will never-ever put the statue of St. Joseph in your bed again."

How you must have loved us, Father, to look beyond our antics and see our desire to serve God. How you must have believed in us to look beyond our inexperience and inadequacies and see what we could become. You helped us to believe in ourselves and you shared your dream with us. We loved being at your side and we could never say "No" to you. Of course that wasn't always good. There are a few more stories that begin with: "Oh sure, Father, I can drive a boat!" or, "Of course I know the way, Father. You just sleep and I'll drive." We'll leave those for another time. As for now, I will simply say I am deeply honored and grateful to have been a part of your dream.

And this brings me to my last promise. You

have asked this of me as long as you have known me. You asked it of me as a volunteer. You asked it of me at my wedding and again at the birth of my children. You asked me to dream. Along with every other volunteer, employee, donor and recipient with whom you've worked, you asked me to look beyond the reality of what is or what isn't, and to dream—with the help of God—impossible dreams.

I will, Father . . . I promise.

Kathleen

EPILOGUE

Today I received a manuscript copy of the book you have in your hands. I went over it, made corrections and additions and changes. As I did, it occurred to me that this may be the last book like this I will write. I reread all the stories and the thoughts and I must confess that I found myself crying. In these pages are people whom I care deeply about—they are my true friends.

I started this book talking about friends and friendship. I want to end it by expressing my feelings for all the friends—all the donors and volunteers and dedicated CAP employees—who have helped me over the years.

Every evening, before I fall asleep, I talk to God. I tell Him the things I meant to do but didn't get around to doing during the day. I apologize for my sins. I ask what new plans He has for me.

I also thank Him for the beauty of His creation. I especially thank Him for His most beautiful creation—His children.

I thank Him for the wonderful people who have supported me these past 45 years . . . I love you all.

I don't love you because you are smart, or attractive, or wealthy. You may be all of those things, but I love you because you are like God.

In giving of your time as volunteers or your money as donors, you are proof that God lives and God loves His children.

The intellect fails, looks fade, and money can disappear as fast as it comes. But the love in your heart that causes you to reach out to your brothers and sisters will only grow and grow.

There will be days in your life when all seems dark . . . when it seems that no one cares, and no one loves you . . . when the loneliness we have all shared since the fall of Eve will seem endless.

On those days I want you to remember — I want you to burn it into your heart — that here in the hills of Appalachia there is a man who loves you and cares about your life and your soul.

I may never meet you, but I will never forget you.

And every night when I talk to God I will ask Him to watch over you, keep you out of harm's way, and shower you with His love.

Our bimonthly magazine, *The Mountain Spirit,* will keep you up-to-date on the work of the Christian Appalachian Project as we continue to help the people of this poverty-stricken area help themselves. In the magazine, you will also find moving, inspiring stories about the people we serve. If you would like to subscribe to this publication (or renew your subscription), please complete the order form below.

THE MOUNTAIN SPIRIT Subscription Order Form

Please enter my one-year subscription to *The Mountain Spirit.* I have enclosed my check for $5.00, made payable to CAP.

Name _____

Address _____

City _____ State _____ Zip _____

Please return this Order Form, along with your check, to: Christian Appalachian Project, 322 Crab Orchard Road, Lancaster, KY 40446

**If You'd Like to
Know More About the
Christian Appalachian Project . . .**

For more information about CAP, or for
additional copies of *Promises to Keep* . . .
. . . *A Vision for Appalachia,* please write or
phone us at our headquarters:

Christian Appalachian Project
322 Crab Orchard Road
Lancaster, KY 40446
(606) 792-3051

Thank you for your interest and support!